W9-AYN-803

Advance praise for *Embracing Motherhood*

"In this small volume, *Embracing Motherhood*, Ms. O'Boyle offers a sensitive reflection on what it means to tune into faith, hope, and charity, living out the vocation of raising children, passing on our Catholic faith, and providing our kids with the necessary roots and wings to live virtuously. Mothers—and fathers too—can grow spiritually from this book, and draw inspiration from her tender perspective. This is a substantive and practical gem as well as an ode of joy for God's gift of motherhood!"
                              —Reverend Timothy M. Dolan, Archbishop of New York

"*Embracing Motherhood* is a delightful read on the joys and challenges of motherhood. Lots of practical parenting tips for raising children in our current culture."
                              —Kimberly Hahn, author of *Legacy of Love:*
                              Biblical Wisdom for Parenting Teens and Young Adults

"Whether you're a Martha or a Mary, whether you have one baby or ten, *Embracing Motherhood* will be a gift to you in your motherly vocation. Donna-Marie Cooper O'Boyle offers a perfect balance of loving wisdom from an experienced Catholic mom's perspective coupled with the jewels of our Church's teachings on family to nurture, support, and encourage you along your path of raising your family in the faith."
                              —Lisa M. Hendey, author of *A Book of Saints for Catholic Moms*

"I can't say enough about *Embracing Motherhood*! Call all your women friends, gather them together and share this extraordinary book. A truly exciting opportunity for individual or small-group enrichment, it contains the best, most engaging discussion questions I have ever seen in a book of this kind. Packed with personal witness and real-life stories of women and their families, this sparkling treasure will move you to tears and bring you great joy. Its nine graceful, accessible chapters include beautiful little prayers by the author that are sure to draw the reader even deeper into contemplation and appreciation for the Church's transcendent wisdom, on a wide variety of topics critical to the health and happiness of Catholic mothers. Donna-Marie Cooper O'Boyle is simply one of the Church's best living resources for women. Her humble, heartfelt work never fails to reach into my soul, as she does in this superb, indispensable manual for mothers."
—Lisa Mladinich, author of *Be an Amazing Catechist: Inspire the Faith of Children*

"In *Embracing Motherhood*, Donna-Marie Cooper O'Boyle does what she does so well: She brings the warm embrace of Christ's love and Church teaching to a point that's accessible and relevant to modern moms. She reaches out across the pages to encourage and challenge women in their unique vocations as mothers."
—Sarah Reinhard, author of *Welcome Baby Jesus* and *Welcome Risen Jesus*

"No stranger to the daily ups and downs of parenting, Cooper O'Boyle uplifts and inspires in *Embracing Motherhood*, showing us how to find and live the extraordinary in the mundane. It's an easy read, filled with Church teaching, personal stories, and practical ideas for turning our homes and daily tasks into places and moments of grace. If every mother and mother-to-be read this book, they would see and feel anew how vitally important their role is in our world; and the world would be a better place for it."
—Vinny Flynn, author of *7 Secrets of the Eucharist*

"One of the greatest blessings with which God has graced me is to have known so many good Catholic mothers. Their strong, steady witness has had a considerable impact on my formation. However, such mothers don't come shrink-wrapped in a package with instructions to 'add water and stir.' Instead, they themselves are formed by their own mothers, other good women, and books like this. It really is the best how-to guide on holy mothering I've ever seen. Hey, Donna! When ya coming out with one for us fathers?"
—Brian O'Neel, author of *Saint Who? 39 Holy Unknowns*

"I get really frustrated when I hear some women say, 'I'm just a mom." Just a mom? What could be more important in this world than saying yes to life and raising up Godly children who will Lord willing, one day grow up to make a difference? In *Embracing Motherhood*, Donna-Marie helps moms realize the beauty, dignity, and long-term impact of their blessed vocation. From years of experience in the 'mom trenches,' Donna-Marie helps moms embrace it all: the diapers, the dance recitals, the dirty dishes, and all of the daily routines that seem ordinary but are truly extraordinary and can lead to great holiness not only for themselves but for their children as well."
—Teresa Tomeo, syndicated Catholic talk-show host

For Nicole~

EMBRACING
Motherhood

DONNA-MARIE COOPER O'BOYLE

Wonderful meeting you!
God bless.
Donna-Marie

SERVANT
BOOKS

PUBLISHED BY ST. ANTHONY MESSENGER PRESS
CINCINNATI, OHIO

Cover and book design by Mark Sullivan
Cover image © Veer | Corbis Photography

LIBRARY OF CONGRESS CATALOGING-IN-PUBLICATION DATA
O'Boyle, Donna-Marie Cooper.
Embracing motherhood / Donna-Marie Cooper O'Boyle.
p. cm.
Includes bibliographical references.
ISBN 978-0-86716-994-2 (pbk. : alk. paper) 1. Mothers—Religious life. 2. Motherhood—Religious aspects—Catholic Church. I. Title.
BX2353.O25 2012
248.8'431—dc23
2011041856

ISBN 978-0-86716-994-2

Published by Servant Books, an imprint of St. Anthony Messenger Press.
28 W. Liberty St.
Cincinnati, OH 45202
www.AmericanCatholic.org
www.ServantBooks.org

Printed in the United States of America.

Printed on acid-free paper.

11 12 13 14 15 5 4 3 2 1

Dedication

For Justin, Chaldea, Jessica, Joseph, and Mary-Catherine,
whose lives have illuminated mine
with endless reasons to embrace
my vocation of motherhood
with all my heart!

CONTENTS

Acknowledgments

With a grateful heart to all my family and friends who have guided me, prayed for me, and loved me throughout my life, especially my parents, Eugene Joseph and Alexandra Mary Cooper, and my brothers and sisters: Alice Jean, Gene, Gary, Barbara, Tim, Michael, and David, I am eternally indebted.

My children have always been my reason for getting up each morning. I love you, Justin, Chaldea, Jessica, Joseph, and Mary-Catherine! My husband, David, the wind beneath my wings, thank you for your love and support! Heartfelt thanks to Cindy Cavnar, Claudia Volkman, and the wonderful team at Servant Books for their partnership in getting this book out!

Loving prayers for all who are connected through my books and talks—thank you for joining me on the journey that leads to LIFE!

Introduction

This book is not about the perfect Catholic family—so you don't have to put it down if you feel yours is imperfect! There are many kinds of families today: traditional two-parent families; single-parent, blended, and foster families; grandparents raising their grandchildren. This is not a book of fluff either. You'll be reading about the realities of a mother's life with all its delights and heart-wrenching circumstances. You'll find, I hope, encouragement, affirmation, and solidarity with someone who has been in the trenches too.

It's not just because I am a mother that I believe the vocation of motherhood is so extraordinary. In fact, I even believe it's a sacred calling like none other. A mother can simply go through the motions in her vocation of motherhood as she strives to keep up with all it entails while trudging through her days, possibly even oblivious to her divine calling. Or, she can fully embrace her vocation, both the joys as well as the sufferings—every bit of it. How many mothers actually *embrace* their vocation? I wonder. How many revel in it all and recognize their role as an actual *vocation*?

Before the Internet and access to countless blogs, a mother used to swap parenting stories while hanging out the laundry as her neighbor leaned in to chat over her back fence. On a big old front porch on a summer afternoon, women used to gab away about family life while their hands crafted family heirlooms and their children played nearby.

Times have changed, haven't they? We seem to run from one event to the next, totally immersed in the task at hand, with little or no thought about our divine purpose. Added to the mix is an unfortunate lack of time to create our own family memories. There's a lot to be said about the ways in which our ancestors mothered. It may appear that I am suggesting we turn back the clocks to an earlier, slower-paced era. No, we live in this present moment in time, and that is where we do our mothering. But I do think we can adopt some practices and wisdom from earlier days.

Where do we learn how to mother anyway? Mothering 101? Obviously, some of our expertise comes to us from our ancestors—our grandmothers, mothers, and maybe our aunts too. We decide what traditions and strategies in mothering we want to carry on and the ones we'd rather leave out. We pick up batches of wisdom and advice along the way from observing other mothers. We gain insight from reading articles or books about Catholic mothering (like the one you have in your hands!). We incorporate what makes sense to us, which practices inspire us, and apply them to our own lives.

And, I hope, we also take some time to pause, ponder, and pray—even if it's only briefly here and there, between tasks or while doing them, so we can hear our Lord's call to us in our mothering. We don't want to allow the current ungodly culture to dictate to us how we should mother our children. That's easy to do as we are bustling around, feeling out of time, and being exposed just about everywhere we look to the nonsense in the media today.

Since most mothers' lives are typically filled to the brim with the care of their household and family as well as with work outside the home, they may seldom have the opportunity to reflect on their lives as mothers and how they are to serve God through their vocation of love. Yet, no matter how much time or inclination a woman has to learn more about becoming a better mother or how to better deal with everything that motherhood entails, the fact remains that, since the beginning of time, motherhood is a vocation filled with the deepest blessings and joys, interwoven with sorrows and challenges. It is a vocation in which a mother is intimately meshed with the human beings who have been entrusted to her care.

I find it pretty incredible to realize that you, Eve, and I have all experienced the miraculous vocation of motherhood. In different ways, of course, yet nonetheless motherhood goes back to the dawn of creation. And as much as mothering practices have changed over the years, the fundamental building blocks of love and service at its core remain the same. A mother's love has to be strong and real enough to be sacrificial, so that for our children's eternal salvation we have to be actually willing to love until it hurts. Bl. Teresa of Calcutta often said that we need to "love until it hurts." We can't answer our Lord with a halfhearted "yes" to our vocation of motherhood. We need to be ready to dive wholeheartedly into it!

I am heartened that Catholic women's study groups are springing up all over where women gather, either through the Internet or—even better—in person at homes or parishes. Women want to learn more about their Catholic faith, and they feel an urge to share their deep interior convictions with other women. A gathering of faithful women can be very healing, loving, and encouraging for all involved.

Women possess many God-given gifts that are meant to be shared. My hope is that, after studying and sharing together, they will also bring those gifts to the world through their love, example, and prayer.

Archbishop Fulton Sheen said, "The history of civilization could actually be written in terms of the level of its women."[1] His sentiment gives us much to think about. Women can actually change history! Let's pray that we women can be instrumental, by God's grace, in creating change in our culture.

Because I know just how busy women are, you're certainly not expected to have *Evangelium Vitae, Mulieris Dignitatem, Familiaris Consortio, Gaudium et Spes*, or even the *Catechism* memorized or readily available in your back pocket or purse or on your night table! I like to weave pertinent Church teaching into my books, articles, and talks to provide essential information to teach, uplift, encourage, and make available to my listeners and readers. For the most part, you won't have to look up a verse or teaching while reading this book. That means you can sit back, enjoy, and absorb.

Down to the nitty-gritty: In *Embracing Motherhood* we will acknowledge that it is not an easy task to raise children in today's culture, and we'll delight in the joys and blessings that are granted to mothers as we usher our children through life, raising our little saints to heaven. We'll also talk about some of the tough subjects that many mothers today are exposed to or are experiencing.

Countless women around the world have shared their woes with me. With their permission, I'm sharing them with you in an effort to aid Catholic mothers striving to work out their salvation within the walls of their domestic church. All the stories in this book are true, but some of the names have been changed to protect identities.

I pray that this book will serve you in your own Catholic mothering and that it may also be a tool with which to help, encourage, and enlighten others when used within a study group. All throughout, you'll explore the numerous facets of motherhood, discovering tools to navigate your rich yet challenging journey so that, equipped with insight and wisdom, you can endeavor to do your job well, please God, and love your children to heaven, while embracing motherhood with all your hearts!

CHAPTER ONE

Blessed With Little Souls

You formed my innermost being.

—Psalm 139:13, *NAB*

GOD GIVES MOTHERS AN AMAZING gift when he blesses them with a unique and unrepeatable new life. Nothing can compare to the exhilaration in a hopeful new mother's heart at the sight of a positive pregnancy test when she has been praying and waiting for that moment. Or to the excitement of a mother who has been eagerly awaiting a new life in her arms through adoption when she receives the news of approval! Mothers all over the world share this common bond of joy about life.

Mothers may consider a pregnancy as a nine-month series of events—a bit (or a lot!) of morning sickness, fatigue, a protruding abdomen, flutters and movements within, and little feet jabbing them in the rib cage. And then, just a little while later, come the

| 1 |

sweet baby coos, peach-fuzz hair, and chubby, dimpled arms and legs that fill the new mother's world.

Bl. John Paul II has said, "In the newborn child is realized the common good of the family." And Bishop Amphilochius, whom Bl. John Paul II quotes in *Evangelium Vitae* (The Gospel of Life), considered the great sacrament of holy matrimony, in which all of what I just described occurs, as "chosen and elevated above all other earthly gifts" and as "the begetter of humanity, the creator of images of God."[1]

We may not think of our babies as "images of God" while we are feeding them, changing their diapers, and totally immersed in their care, but they, in fact, are! Bl. John Paul II reminds us: "Thus, a man and woman joined in matrimony become partners in a divine undertaking: through the act of procreation, God's gift is accepted and a new life opens to the future."[2]

I have often expressed that there is no greater gift than to be able to cooperate with God to bring life into the world. Babies are an incredible gift of God's love coming to us within the loving marital embrace, or through the gift of adoption. Sometimes I think that women forget that it's never our *right* to have a child. A child is God's *gift* to us.

What does the Church teach us about our responsibility as Catholics to be open to new life? I'll cite just a few examples here, but there are plenty more. Let's start at the beginning. In Genesis we are told, "God blessed them, and God said to them, 'Be fruitful and multiply, and fill the earth and subdue it'" (Genesis 1:28). As well, we learn from Genesis, "When God created humankind, he made them in the likeness of God. Male and female he created them, and he blessed them and named them 'Humankind' when they were created" (Genesis 5:1–2, *NRSV*).

Not every Pre-Cana conference or marriage-preparation class gives the accurate teaching of the Church in this regard. I remember vividly that at the Pre-Cana conference I attended, we were all told that "family planning is between your doctor and you." Even though I was a young twentysomething at the time, it didn't take long before I figured out that the conference people were in error. But not everyone may realize this. After all, when we participate in a Church-sponsored teaching event, we expect, well, Church teaching, which sadly is not always the case.

The *Catechism of the Catholic Church* (which I'll later refer to as "*CCC*" or "the *Catechism*") instructs us:

> So the Church, which "is on the side of life" teaches that "each and every marriage act must remain open to the transmission of life." This particular doctrine, expounded upon on numerous occasions by the Magisterium, is based on the inseparable connection, established by God, which man on his own initiative may not break, between the unitive significance and the procreative significance which are both inherent to the marriage act.[3]

The Church has forever been in favor of defending life against all attacks, in "whatever condition or state of development it is found."[4] I highly recommend that you get your hands on a copy of *Familiaris Consortio*, this apostolic exhortation by Bl. John Paul II, and read it in its entirety. Many essential teachings about the transmission of human life and the husband and wife's cooperation are covered in it. You can find it at Catholic bookstores or on the Vatican website at http://www.vatican.va.

My mother told me that she was teased quite a bit by her peers because she had eight children. "Haven't you heard of birth control?" some would heartlessly ask, while slinging other opinions about procreation her way. Her doctor even advised her not to have so many children. I, for one, baby number seven, am happy my mother didn't listen to the culture dictating to her what she should or should not do in terms of welcoming new life. God bless my mother and mothers everywhere!

I too have heard from many who offered—or perhaps I should say "pushed"—their personal opinions on me regarding what size my family should be. My own Catholic doctor recommended that I get my tubes tied. If I had listened to him, Mary-Catherine wouldn't be here today. If I had listened to the opinions of others, I may have had only one child (since my first was an emergency C-section) and I would have never experienced a rich family life filled with everything motherhood entails. In addition, my children would have missed the experience of growing up in a larger family.

If we still need more concrete instruction concerning our responsibility to be open to life, Mother Church in the *Catechism* tells us: "Called to give life, spouses share in the creative power and fatherhood of God (cf. Ephesians 3:14; Matthew 23:9). 'Married couples should regard it as their proper mission to transmit human life and to educate their children; they should realize that they are thereby cooperating with the love of God the Creator and are, in a certain sense, its interpreters. They will fulfill this duty with a sense of human and Christian responsibility.'"[5]

Recognizing and understanding that, through the sacrament of marriage, spouses "share in the creative power and fatherhood of God" should actually make us ecstatically joyful! Taking time to ponder and pray about that important and inseparable spiritual element of the marital embrace will enrich and bless our lives and marriages incredibly. We should always endeavor to call on the graces of the sacrament of marriage whenever we can. God is forever present to us in our vocation as a mother and wife.

Birth Control

One of the biggest issues that separate Catholics from our Protestant brothers and sisters is artificial birth control, which the Catholic Church does not permit and considers intrinsically evil. What is wrong with artificial birth control? Why shouldn't couples be allowed to hold off having children or be able to space them out?

Couples may think that using birth control merely prevents a conception. In reality, it actually harms the marriage because the couple is not totally opening themselves up to one another. It may even terminate a new human life, as is the case with certain birth-control methods and certain types of birth-control pills. Several types of pills and methods act as abortifacients, making the woman's body uninhabitable for the newly fertilized egg. It is designed to make the body sick, in a sense. Some types cause the body to do something abnormal: prevent ovulation, so that an egg is never released to be fertilized. The pill also subjects some high-risk women to many serious side effects, including stroke and heart attack.

We live, as Bl. John Paul wrote in *Familiaris Consortio,* in a "culture which seriously distorts or entirely misinterprets the true meaning of human sexuality because it separates it from its essential reference to the person."[6] The Church teaches that the conjugal act (the marital embrace) holds two meanings: the unitive meaning and the procreative meaning. If the two meanings are separated by contraception, then the couple has manipulated and degraded human sexuality—"and with it themselves and their married partner—by altering its value of 'total' self-giving."[7] Using contraception, then, is not only a couple's refusal to be open to human life, but it is also a refusal to totally give oneself to one's spouse.

Our culture suggests that it is completely fine and even advisable to use contraception, conveying the idea that procreation is merely a biological act. The Church, on the other hand, sees the marital act as something that involves the whole person—body, mind, and soul. Our culture even advocates that we have a responsibility to our planet to limit our offspring because the world is supposedly becoming overpopulated. Some ecologists and futurologists have caused a kind of panic with their exaggerations, and a couple's fears about bringing children into a cruel, heartless world are then increased. Another reason couples put off starting families is that they are preoccupied with acquiring material goods and fail to open their hearts to the spiritually rich gift of human life.

Many couples also fear the ongoing struggle they may face financially in raising several children in our world today. They may be exposed to the messages of the mass media, which present perpetual images of huge houses, small families, and much material wealth, which then becomes the norm to be achieved. If you see it enough in the media and experience it through friends and acquaintances, that sort of lifestyle can become more and more alluring. Pope John Paul II explains that "excessive prosperity and the consumer mentality, paradoxically joined to a certain anguish and uncertainty about the future, deprive married couples of the generosity and courage needed for raising up new human life: thus life is often perceived not as a blessing, but as a danger from which to defend oneself."[8]

Other fears enter the picture as well. Many couples have come from broken homes themselves and may doubt their ability to stay committed for a lifetime and to parent well. It would make sense to pray for generosity and courage so that we may follow God's holy will regarding our openness to human life. Our Lord will grant us the graces we need. We have to ask, though!

Family Planning

The Church instructs us that "each and every marriage act must remain open to the transmission of life."[9] We are meant to have an attitude of openness. Because a Catholic married couple has been given a mission by God to "transmit human life and to educate their children" and "fulfill this duty with a sense of human and Christian responsibility," let's talk about what is permitted in family planning.[10]

The Church teaches that there are times when it is all right to space out the conception of our children. Specifically, the *Catechism* says: "For just reasons, spouses may wish to space the births of their children. It is their duty to make certain that their desire is not motivated by selfishness but is in conformity with the generosity appropriate to responsible parenthood. Moreover, they should conform their behavior to the objective criteria of morality."[11]

A couple may wish to wait to have children because they feel they need to accomplish various things on a practical level before bringing a family into the world. While their desires may not necessarily come from a selfish heart, they may be misguided nonetheless.

"Just reasons" would not include a situation in which a married couple wants to hold off on conceiving children because they want to save money to buy their dream house. It also does not include putting off having children so they can build up their bank account.

The *Catechism* instructs us that making the right decision about having children at a particular time does not only depend on our "sincere intention" and "evaluation of motives." We are told that our decisions in this regard "must be determined by objective criteria, criteria drawn from the nature of the person and his acts, criteria that respect the total meaning of mutual self-giving and human procreation in the context of true love; this is possible only if the virtue of married chastity is practiced with sincerity of heart."[12] I always advise couples to learn about natural family planning (NFP) *before* they are married. Engaged couples can take classes before marriage to become familiar with the body's signs and to learn about fertile and infertile times. Pope Paul VI told us in *Humanae Vitae* that sometimes physical and psychological reasons come into play when spacing out births. Specifically he said, "If there are serious motives to space out births, which derive from physical or psychological conditions of husband or wife, or from external conditions, it is licit to take account of the natural rhythms inherent in the generative functions."[13]

Ultimately, God is the author of life. He blesses a couple with a child when it fits into his divine will. God certainly has a perfect design for our lives, and he is in charge. Our part is to pray for an openness to life. I speak about the Church's teachings on openness to life in my book *The Domestic Church Room by Room: A Mother's Study Guide* (Servant Books). In chapter 3, "The Nursery," I recommend that the engaged or married couple seek out classes taught by a qualified instructor in natural family planning who is approved by the Church. I also encourage couples to read the *Catechism* together, in particular section 2360, in the subarticle "The Love of Husband and Wife," as well as relevant Church documents such as *Casti Connubii* (Christian Marriage) by Pope Pius XI, *Humanae Vitae* by Pope Paul VI, and *Familiaris Consortio, Mulieris Dignitatem,* and *Evangelium Vitae* by Blessed John Paul II (available on the Vatican website, http://www.vatican.va) to further understand the Church's teachings on Christian family life.

Caring for Our Brood

Bl. John Paul II wrote in *Mulieris Dignitatem* that, although human parenthood is usually shared by both parents,

> *the woman's motherhood constitutes a special "part" in this shared parenthood*, and the most demanding part. Parenthood—even though it belongs to both—is realized much more fully in the woman, especially in the prenatal period. It is the woman who "pays" directly for this shared generation, which literally absorbs the energies of her body and soul. It is therefore that *the man* be fully aware that in their shared parenthood he *owes a special debt to the woman*.

No programme of "equal rights" between women and men
is valid unless it takes this fact fully into account.[14]

Bravo, Bl. John Paul II! He really knew how to get to the heart of
the matter! He truly understood the heart of a woman. It's nice to
know that at least one man (other than our Lord Jesus) understood
the sweat and blood of motherhood. His statement regarding man's
"special debt" to women is heartening as well. We're not going to
expect an extra pat on the back from the men who "owe a special
debt"—or anyone else, for that matter—for our loving efforts in the
family. But it's sure nice knowing that our Church understands.

Pope Benedict XVI has also acknowledged the love and care of
mothers and wives and has highlighted the beauty of the sacrament
of marriage. "My thanks," he said, "to so many women who, day after
day, still light up their families through their witness of Christian
life. May the Spirit of the Lord inspire, even today, the sanctity of
Christian couples to show the world the beauty of marriage lived
according to gospel values."[15] I really like the image of *lighting up*
our families!

You may find it very interesting to learn, as I did, that new mothers
actually grow bigger brains after giving birth! Sounds incredible,
doesn't it? However, new research published in *Behavioral
Neuroscience* explained that MRI brain scans of women before and
after birth revealed that the new mothers had developed additional
gray matter in the areas of the brain relating to maternal motivation,
reward and emotion processing, sensory integration, and reasoning
and judgment. In addition, the mothers who were most excited
about their new babies were significantly more likely to grow larger
midbrains.[16]

Influencing One Another

Did you ever pause to consider that as you raise your children, they are in a sense "raising" you too? Think about it. Where would you be now if you weren't mothering your child (or children)? What other choices might you have made if you weren't compelled to remain on the straight and narrow road to heaven because of the children in your life? It's very possible that you could have veered off the path because of poor or selfish choices. Being a parent prods us to be selfless and focused on the welfare of our children. I believe that our hearts grow with each child. Each child teaches us to love more, if that could be possible. God has it all figured out!

Bl. John Paul II explained in *Familiaris Consortio* that while our children grow "in wisdom and in stature, and in favor with God and man, [they] offer their own precious contribution to building of the family community and even the sanctification of their parents."[17] This certainly gives us another way to look on the joyful times and also the challenges and struggles that beset us in the household, including sibling rivalry, teenage issues, and growing pains. Family life is a means to sanctification for all. Our response to the happenings of family life is the very stuff that affects us for better or for worse and ultimately determines our spiritual health.

We are helped to grow in virtue and holiness as we raise our children. As we practice spiritual and corporal works of virtue in the household, we learn patience, perseverance, humility, and charity. In a sense, our children become the "least of these our brothers" as we clothe them, feed them, and care for them (see Matthew 25:31–46).

Once, when my son, Justin, was young, he must have sensed some tension in the air. He stood between my husband and me when we were deep in a discussion. In a very "priestly" voice (we had just come home from Mass), Justin said, "Peace be with you!" It stopped us in our tracks and, although it made us smile, it gave us something very important to think about. Our children have much to teach us every day, whether it's some nugget of wisdom woven into their conversations with us, the radiance of their beautiful innocence, or their splendid, childlike abandon to life. So much happens within the walls of our homes! Our domestic church becomes the place where we learn to love and forgive and patiently endure sacrifices for one another, all the while helping to pave the way to heaven for our family members—and for ourselves too!

Our loving responses in a myriad of situations help to transform and bring peace to troubled or weary hearts. Even household drudgery can become wonderful occasions for prayer. I have always found this whole concept to be so amazing while making complete sense too—we help to sanctify one another through our love for one another in our domestic churches. Amazing!

Working Outside the Home

It's wise to consider how we will raise our children *before* we are married. I suggest that engaged couples talk openly about the care of the children and the chores in the home so that they can establish some groundwork for a plan together. We all are aware that it's difficult these days to operate a household on one income, and because of this there always seems to be a huge struggle for the woman in deciding if she should work outside the home or not. Not all women have a choice in this matter, for a variety of reasons: Some may be single mothers or may be struggling financially because their husbands' income doesn't cover the necessary household expenses. Women may consider their role in the home insignificant, or they may not feel the recognition due them for their hard work. There won't be many words of affirmation from tiny babies and little ones. You can expect to receive instead, without a doubt, sleepless nights, changing countless dirty diapers, picking up after toddlers who leave a trail behind them, and much more. But let's not forget the beautiful smiles, giggles, and warmest of hugs!

We women are very talented and can do many things. Yet all motives for working outside the home should be pondered thoroughly. I think the most important factor in this considerable decision should be *when* even more than *if*. *When* is the right time to leave your children to the care of another while you work outside the home? Discerning that answer will take much thought, prayer, and communication with your husband or, if you don't have a husband, a close friend or family member.

If a couple sincerely discuss their needs and desires for raising their family and carefully and selflessly consider their children's needs above their own, they will be OK. The key words here are *sincerely*, *carefully*, and *selflessly*. They must keep at the forefront of all of their decisions that their children deserve a parents' presence if at all possible, instead of having someone else raise them. Long periods of time when you are absent from your children does translate to "someone else raising them." Therefore, you will want to enlist a loving relative or someone you know who takes a special interest in your child's welfare and shares your values in caring for your children if you are not able to be there all of the time.

Perhaps there are creative ways to generate an income from home or at least do some of your work from home. The workplace is definitely changing; these days there are many options for job-sharing and telecommuting, for instance. Sacrifices are required to juggle everyone's schedules. But *sacrifice* is really a parent's middle name. This is a time to pray, ponder, and discern. The culture presents all of the things you *need* to possess and why you *need* to have another income to support these things. We really have to turn to the Lord. Each situation is unique; however, the very best scenario is for us to be present to our children.

I chose to stay home and raise my kids because I felt it was the most important thing for me to do—I chose to put any other desire or pursuit I might have had aside while I cared for them. I made the *decision* to stay home to be present to my children. It was not a *luxury,* as some might think. I lived with a lot less of the material comfort to be there for my family. I am not here to judge any mother for her choices or to cause her to feel pangs of guilt because of her decisions, especially when it's difficult for her to leave her children and go off to work. I am here to offer—sister-to-sister, woman-to-woman—what I feel may help other mothers think through these important issues.

Children grow up so quickly! The ages of my own five children attest to that. Each year when my oldest child, Justin, has yet another birthday, I always say, "What? How did he get to be that old?" That's one of the reasons I try my best to encourage mothers to be there for their children. They grow up in a flash, and you don't want to miss it or look back and regret that you weren't a part of it. You want to know that you gave your children all you could possibly give.

R E F L E C T I O N

Do you spend too much time away from your young children and therefore allow others to care for them, others who may not have your Christian beliefs? Are there any other options open to you? Talk to the Lord in prayer about this.

Pray for the grace to be open to life, whatever that may mean to you at your stage of life.

Where do you find yourself struggling?

Are there any Church teachings you have a hard time accepting? Will you pray about this?

A P R A Y E R F O R T H E J O U R N E Y

O Lord, help me to be open to your holy will in my life. Please grant me the graces, courage, and generosity needed as a mother responsible for welcoming life and nurturing it within my domestic church. Blessed Mother Mary, please guide me each day in my mothering. Amen.

Building Our Domestic Church

> Marriage is an act of will that signifies and involves a
> mutual gift, which unites the spouses and binds them
> to their eventual souls, with whom they make up a sole
> family—a domestic church.
>
> —Bl. John Paul II

I LOVE THAT OUR HOME is a little domestic church—an oasis to retreat
to from the craziness of the world. As mothers, being the heart of
the home, we have the responsibility of creating our own domestic
church. It should be a place where all feel welcome and secure—a
safe haven. Sure, there will be occasional growing pains and sibling
rivalry as you all work out your salvation together in the blessedness
of the family—in your little church. But all in all, it is a holy and
sacred place, really and truly! Of course, we have to make it that
way; it doesn't just happen by itself. We are the creators of our
domestic churches, with God's help—cocreators with him.

I knew long ago that my home would never be "aesthetically correct." Naturally, I wanted my house to be clean and orderly, but I came to a point where I recognized it would never be "perfect." Because people come first in my house, I can't expect the entire household to be sparkling clean or up-to-date at every moment.

As you're taking care of your little ones or relishing the joy of playing with them, don't feel guilty that there may be a light layer of dust on the bookshelf nearby. You'll get to it eventually. Don't worry if your furniture is on the shabby side. Put your heart at ease—you can't expect perfection, not in this lifetime anyway. Life in a busy family doesn't always afford time or finances to have everything just so. Don't put undue pressure on yourself.

You may be familiar with the expression, "If Mama ain't happy, ain't nobody happy." Let's keep this in mind as we strive to build for our families a beautiful domestic church where memories are created and family love can flourish. Let's pray for a real joy of heart that will transcend to our family members, giving them a safe, warm, nurturing environment in which to grow.

We can try our best to follow these directives from Ephesians: "Get rid of all bitterness, all passion and anger, harsh words, slander, and malice of every kind. In place of these, be kind to one another, compassionate, and mutually forgiving, just as God has forgiven you in Christ" (Ephesians 4:31–32).

Whether our domestic church is a huge, beautifully decorated house, a little bungalow, a modest apartment, or even a hut in a developing country, a mother's love there at its heart will help her spouse and children to survive and grow in the blessedness of their family.

Blessed Mother Teresa once told a story that touched my heart. It was about a mother's love. A small girl was wandering around, searching through the rubble of the streets of Calcutta, India, for food to fill her hungry belly. The Missionary of Charity sisters who, along with Mother Teresa, came upon her, took her to their orphanage and cared for her, giving her clean clothes, food to eat, and a warm shelter. After a few days, the girl went missing. The sisters searched for the her and finally found her under the shade of a tree with her mother and siblings. That tree was her home, where she basked in the love of her mother and family. She chose a home with no walls and sparse food in order to be with her mother and family. A mother's love is powerful!

The *Catechism* explains: "The Christian home is the place where children receive the first proclamation of the faith. For this reason the family home is rightly called 'the domestic church,' a community of grace and prayer, a school of human virtues and of Christian charity."[1]

In *Evangelium Vitae*, Bl. John Paul II wrote: "As the domestic church, the family is summoned to proclaim, celebrate, and serve the Gospel of life. This is a responsibility which first concerns married couples, called to be givers of life, on the basis of an ever greater awareness of the meaning of procreation as a unique event which clearly reveals that human life is a gift received in order then to be given as a gift. In giving origin to a new life, parents recognize that the child 'as the fruit of their mutual gift of love, is in turn, a gift for both of them, a gift flows from them.'"[2]

Pope Benedict XVI tells us, "Every home is called to become a 'domestic church' in which family life is completely centered on the lordship of Christ and the love of husband and wife mirrors the mystery of Christ's love for the Church, his bride."[3]

This is a very tall order! I wonder how many homes are "completely centered on the lordship of Christ." How many marriages "mirror the mystery of Christ's love for the Church"? As unobtainable as that goal may sometimes seem, it is very doable one step at a time. Key words here: "one step at a time." We'll find that God certainly makes up for what is lacking in us if we offer him our desiring hearts and continue to strive each day to come closer to him.

A domestic church starts with a stable Christian marriage. The unity of husband and wife is required to create a loving Christian home. Throughout the day-to-day life of raising their family, the husband and wife actually create a blessed "community of grace and prayer, a school of human virtues and of Christian charity." I don't have to tell you that each family home may not exactly look like a page out of the *Catechism*. We certainly fail to mirror Christ's love at times—we make mistakes, even many times. But we shouldn't give up because of our shortcomings. We can seek forgiveness and healing, and we can pray for strength and guidance to be a living example of God's love in our marriages and in our families. Throughout our self-emptying journey in marriage, our love grows stronger and deeper as we begin each day anew.

And all the while, we can pray for the graces to fulfill our duties in a way that is pleasing to God and show the world the dignity of the sacrament of matrimony. The Church teaches us that "the sacrament of matrimony signifies the union of Christ and the Church. It gives spouses the grace to love each other with the love with which Christ has loved his Church; the grace of the sacrament thus perfects the human love of the spouses, strengthens their indissoluble unity, and sanctifies them on the way to eternal life."[4]

The Feminine Genius of the Home

I truly believe that the road to heaven is paved with *give and take* but mostly *give*. We are called to be very flexible, loving, and patient in our dealings with our husbands and children—give and take. The *taking* part is in accepting them, their love as well as their idiosyncrasies.

With regard to our dear "other half," we must come to recognize that, in essence, we hold our husband's hearts in our hands. I don't think we fully understand the degree of power we possess. God has given us many beautiful gifts, and he expects that we will use them for the betterment of our marriage and our family. If we want our husbands to be the man of the house—to protect us and love us with tenderness—we have to love them enough to allow them to *be* that man. Wives have to loosen their grip and show respect to their husbands.

You need to recognize that even a look of disdain from you will affect your husband's psyche. You have the power to raise him up or tear him down. If you want your spouse to grow into the role our Lord has for him as head of the family, compliment him, uplift him, communicate honestly with him, and lead him to God with your love and your prayers. Be there for him—be present both physically and emotionally. He wants to please you, and he absolutely needs your affirmation.

Men can be misguided by the culture too and might be tempted to assume a different role, something rather distorted. It's up to us as wives to encourage our husbands in their God-given role as men. Aside from our love, affirmation, and encouragement, the most important thing we can do for our husbands is to be patient with them and to pray for them. We can ask dear St. Joseph to help our husbands. The rosary is a powerful prayer we can pray for them, and for ourselves too. Let's pray to become more awakened to our own personal gifts and feminine genius.

In addition to the ways in which the culture negatively influences men, we must be aware of the raging spiritual battle that has been going on ever since the dawn of creation. Some may wish to believe this is not so. However, I am telling you right now, it's indeed true. We have to be aware that marriage is always under attack. We must not fall prey to the workings of the evil one. The *Catechism* tells us: "Every man experiences evil around him and within himself. This experience makes itself felt in the relationships between man and woman."[5] It goes on to tell us that a disorder of discord, a spirit of domination, infidelity, jealousy, and conflict can manifest and that couples need to call on God's grace "to heal the wounds of sin."[6] God's infinite mercy will never refuse them. "Without his help man and woman cannot achieve the union of their lives for which God created them 'in the beginning.'"[7] Prayer is the weapon to combat the evil one's workings—pray as a couple and ask God to grant you the graces you need.

Bl. Teresa of Calcutta said, "We must make our homes centers of compassion and forgive endlessly."[8] This is a challenging task for a worn-out mother, yet it surely is the secret to happiness in our families. We must consistently give with love and forgiveness if we want to know real peace in our hearts and see God at work in our homes.

The Christian wife is the heart of the home; she is the parent who has been gifted with a heart that seeks to care for her offspring even through sacrifice. She is the parent who usually has the most immediate hands-on care of the children. She "feathers her nest," as my husband calls it, by decorating her home, making it a pleasant place to be. She can start traditions for her family and carry on traditions from hers and her husband's past.

A single mother who does not have the help of a husband to raise the children can deepen her own faith to be able to prayerfully create her domestic church and pass on her faith to her children. I was a single mom for many years, so I intimately realize the great struggles and difficulties in raising children alone. With God, I persevered. He showed me that I was not alone after all.

We are not going to find perfection in the family in this lifetime. But we can strive for it, absolutely, while always keeping in mind that our lives within our domestic churches are works in progress. We can't expect to build a grand cathedral in a day! With God's grace and help and our desiring heart, we are heading in the right direction. Next, let's look at some tangible ways we can build up our domestic church.

The Dinner Table

"The best and surest way to learn the love of Jesus," Bl. Teresa of Calcutta said, "is through the family."[9] In our everyday dealings with the family, we can surely experience the love of Jesus. I am convinced that amazing things happen when families gather at the end of the day to break bread together—to reconnect and grow as a family. Dinnertime is a lot more than just filling our bellies.

I'm immensely appreciative that my mother saw the importance of mealtimes together, and because she did, she passed down vital traditions to my siblings and me. We all ate together at the dinner table, not in front of the television set. Our dinner conversations may not have always been profound, and our behavior at times may not have been Norman Rockwell picture-perfect (far from it), but we were, without doubt, growing together and learning from one another and, what is maybe even more important, were provided with an invaluable paradigm.

How can we create fond memories and have meaningful conversations if we are talking on our cell phones, playing electronic games, or watching TV? We must lay down the law—no phones or games at the dinner table, no texting when conversing within the family setting.

Spilled drinks, arguments, or kids in a rush to leave the dinner table may hardly look like an occasion for grace and prayer. We can't expect impeccable behavior and impeccable dinners together, especially when our children are young. Accidents happen, kids get messy, adults lose patience, or a teen may be having a hard day. Parents are wise to lower their expectations while still teaching their children to respect them and practice good manners as best they can. Everything in the family is a learning process! This is where tenderness, forgiveness, respect, fidelity, and more come in, as parents strive to fulfill their responsibility to educate their children.

Even amid the occasionally chaotic mealtimes, families forge a blessed bond together while creating lasting memories. We may sometimes need to remind ourselves that we live within a family, not a regimented military mess hall. Flexibility and patience are paramount. Rigidity often causes butting of heads and disappointment because of expectations of results that may be unobtainable at that moment—results beyond one's abilities. However, we certainly can expect that cell phones, iPods, electronic games, and other kinds of technology should not be at the dinner table. It's tough enough to keep our children's attention when they're not distracted, and we don't need unnecessary competition when we're attempting to have a nice meal together.

Technology isn't the only distraction either. If my husband happens to pick up the newspaper to glance at the news as I put dinner on the table, I teasingly call him "Ricky Ricardo"—he gets the point and puts the paper away. Remember the *I Love Lucy* show? Lucy was forever frustrated with her husband Ricky for reading the newspaper at the table. We have to make sure that we consider each other important enough to want to sit down together. Dinnertime is a time not just to scarf down food but to communicate and share our hearts.

In the introduction of this book, I alluded to the beauty in the simplicity of earlier days, not to suggest that we regress but to understand the importance of not getting caught up in modern technology to the extent that it takes over our lives and even interferes with our relationship with God. With that in mind, we mothers need to set the boundaries and expectations with our families and stick with them. Yes, we may not be popular all of the time, but that's a sacrifice we make because of our love for our families.

Beginning your meal with prayer sets the tone. Grace before meals prayer can be said together, followed by an Our Father and a Hail Mary while you have your captive audience. There's no need to worry if your little ones don't get the prayers just right, as long as they try. The littlest ones will just listen (or so we hope). Prayers voiced from your united hearts are very pleasing to God. I often like to add a few special intentions to that short prayer time. Your children can chime in too—asking God to help a friend, a relative, or a pet.

In just a few moments' time, you will have united yourselves in prayer before God and placed yourselves under Blessed Mother Mary's mantle. You also will have started a tradition of gathering around the family table for prayer, a tradition that you may hope will make its way into your children's future domestic churches. And to think, you would miss out on this amazing opportunity for grace if you didn't introduce prayer at the dinner table. Seize the moment—get your family praying! It's best to get them started as young as possible. Don't worry about a spilled drink or an upset. Take a breath, compose yourself, and carry on. Our Lord is there with you. Invite him to be an expected guest at your table.

One time a young teen visited my home, along with her family. This young lady walked into the dining room when I was setting the table for lunch. As I placed the silverware on the table, she asked, "Do you always set the table like that?" I paused a second, pondering what she may have meant, and responded with a question. "Yes, we are going to have a meal together, aren't we?" She proceeded to tell me that her family doesn't sit at the table very often—"hardly ever," she told me. She said they eat in front of the television set, at the computer, or at different times from one another. I offered up a quick prayer for her and her family, hoping that maybe the example of all of us eating together at the table would inspire this family to do the same. Sadly, she didn't feel that sense of *celebration* in her own family. Those of us who do sit at the family dinner table together can be an example to others who don't live in homes where their family pauses to enjoy time together—chaos and all!

I find it sad to think that sitting down to dinner as a family is becoming almost obsolete in many families. In addition to families being uninterested in sitting down to a meal together, many families these days are so busy that their schedules are packed to the brim. Many parents are running themselves ragged trying to keep up with the unrealistic demands of sports practices and kids' activities. When they are chasing after all of those other pursuits, they fail to see that they are forgetting about their first priority: raising their family close to the hearth and home. Our kids *should* be well-rounded in sports, the arts, and other extracurricular activities. As parents we must be sure, however, that we are not allowing the culture to raise our kids by taking them away from the home and our presence so often. We may have to cut back on a troublesome schedule so we can enjoy family dinners together, keeping in mind that it is at the table together that we reconnect after a long day, where we communicate and grow as a family, and where we grow together in faith as well. We set an example for others too in keeping a strong commitment to our family dinnertimes. This might come up in conversation when you are explaining to another parent why you won't be signing your child up for a particular activity that will interfere too often with dinnertime.

When I was a little girl, being home for dinner was not merely a suggestion. It was a requirement. All eight of us kids knew that come "hell or high water," you were home for dinner on time. (Actually, we called it "supper" back then. Somehow, I got around to calling this evening meal *dinner* later, when I became more "sophisticated.") I also recall happy memories of going to dinner at other homes. We often had get-togethers at relatives' homes. Sunday was a typical day for us to visit or have relatives visit us. I have fond memories of my grandmother sitting with us kids, grating a mound of potatoes for her famous potato pancakes or mixing ingredients for her delicious Polish cookies.

I savor vivid memories of getting together for dinner at my friend Angela's home. She also lived in Ridgefield, Connecticut, where I grew up. We got together regularly. If I happened to be visiting her near a mealtime, her gracious family would add another place setting to the table and encourage me to join them for dinner. Without too much coaxing, I would agree, and we would enjoy a home-cooked family meal together in the simplicity of their kitchen. I felt warmly welcomed in their home and at their table. They radiated a beautiful example of Christian charity, of being a close-knit Catholic family who recognized the importance of gathering together at the table even when it was only for leftovers. Both Angela and I now have large families of our own, and we frequently add an extra place setting for an unexpected guest in our own homes.

Let's make our mealtimes happy times for the whole family by putting extra care into how we set the table and plan our meals. Let's be sure to include prayer and wholesome conversation while we are together. Dinnertime then transforms into a memorable time for us together as a family, nourishing our minds and souls as well as our bodies.

Sacred Images and a Prayer Corner

We are touched by beauty. Over the years people have remarked that walking into my home is like walking into a church. I understand what they mean. They observe the many sacred images that adorn the walls in every room of my house, items that perhaps they aren't accustomed to seeing in an ordinary home. I will admit that my humble little office where I do my writing and radio shows resembles a shrine to the saints! I can't help it—the sacred draws me in. I am comforted by having icons, statues, and sacramentals around me. Many of them have been blessed, bringing an extra richness to me. I feel prodded interiorly to pray when I see them. In the same way, Catholic parents can utilize sacred images in their own domestic churches to focus more attention on what is sacred and less on what is worldly.

Begin opening your home to holiness by inviting your parish priest over to bless your domestic church, whether it is an apartment or a house. A holy water font can be placed inside the front door so holy water is always readily available and is a reminder of our baptism. A St. Benedict medal, about the size of a silver dollar, hangs above my front door in the foyer as a protection for my home; this medal holds a powerful exorcism prayer guarding against evil. Each bedroom in your home should have at least a crucifix on the wall above the bed or in some visible spot. Children can be taught to kneel at their bedside in the morning and at night to say their prayers. I still have the crucifix that was in my room when I was a child. I came across it a while back, cleaned it up, and hung it above my bed. Although it's a little bit marred and chipped, it's a poignant reminder to me of the presence of my loving God, one who has been with me my whole life, whether I knew it totally or not.

A patron saint's image or another piece of religious art fits nicely on a wall in a child's room. A framed prayer or blessing works well in the dining room or kitchen. On my dining room wall is a beautiful painting of the Blessed Mother holding Baby Jesus which formerly hung in the dining room of my dear friend and former spiritual director (now deceased), Fr. Bill Smith.

Your living room is a great place to hang an image of the Sacred Heart of Jesus or the Immaculate Heart of Mary. In addition to these images in my dining room, in my living room hangs a beautiful yet simple black-and-white framed picture of the Sacred Heart of Jesus. I found it in a thrift store years ago and walked out of there smiling from ear to ear after paying a whole two dollars for it! This picture has graced the wall of my living room (wherever I lived) ever since, bringing me a feeling of peace whenever I gaze on it. Trust me, I have knelt before this image more times than I can count—when in dire need, or simply after closing the front door after my family has left for school or work as I implore Jesus' loving, merciful Sacred Heart for his help and safety for them.

These sacred images throughout our domestic churches are much more than flat pictures on a wall or sculpted piles of clay. Rather, they represent and in a sense bring to life Jesus, Mary, or the saints, with whom we can communicate in a special way—on our knees or from our hearts—as we traipse from room to room in our homes throughout the day, caring for our kids or doing our domestic chores. Sacred images help our family members to keep their eyes lifted upward even amid the ordinary stuff that goes on in family life. For instance, the kids are playing games on the floor, and nearby is a basket of rosary beads, and a statue of the Blessed Mother, whose baby Jesus fills her arms, decorates the mantle over the fireplace. Crucifixes showing us the real definition of love adorn walls, and Catholic and Christian books fill bookshelves. Worship, sacred, and classical music can fill the house with a beautiful, calming ambiance. This way, the sacred will become familiar as the children grow; it will be comfortable and comforting. This recollection will stay with them, even if they should decide to stray from the straight and narrow path later in life. It will pull them back, along with a parent's powerful prayers.

In my dining room a small table is positioned under the beautiful painting of the Blessed Mother, and here I have placed various sacred objects. It's an area in my home where one can go and be inspired, say a prayer, or just gaze on the objects there. It can be a place to gather to light an Advent wreath, read a Bible story, or pray a decade of the rosary together.

You can easily create a prayer table in your own home. Pick an area, even if it's just a small corner, and simply place religious objects on the table: a basket of rosary beads, a bottle of holy water, and perhaps an occasional vase of fresh flowers to celebrate special feast days or holy days. You may choose to have a candle or candles atop the table, perhaps lit (with adult supervision) during a prayer time. You can also burn incense on holy days to make your prayer more ceremonious. An icon or painting can be hung above the table.

Be creative. You can change it up according to the liturgical seasons or your own tastes. My prayer corner has always been kid-friendly—I have children's Bible stories and books handy as well as colorful rosary beads, crayons, and saints' coloring pages. I'm sure I don't need to remind you that any objects that are accessible to small children should be safe and used with supervision. As the kids grow, you can swap out the kids' beads for grown-up ones, and children's stories for ones that are more mature. Use your prayer table or corner to draw your family closer to God by making the sacred familiar and *touchable*.

Hanging beneath the images of the Immaculate Heart of Mary and the Sacred Heart of Jesus that grace the wall of my dining room is this framed prayer:

Act of Family Consecration

Most Sacred Heart of Jesus and Immaculate Heart of Mary, we consecrate ourselves and our entire family to You. We consecrate to You: our very being and all our life, all that we are, all that we have, and all that we love. To You we give our bodies, our hearts, and our souls. To You we dedicate our home and our country. Mindful of this consecration, we promise You to live the Christian way by the practice of Christian virtues, with great regard for respect for one another. O Most Sacred Heart of Jesus and Immaculate Heart of Mary, accept our humble confidence and this act of consecration by which we entrust ourselves and all our family to You. Most Sacred Heart of Jesus, have mercy on us. Immaculate Heart of Mary, pray for us.

REFLECTION

Do you look for Jesus' love in your everyday dealings with the family? What are some examples?

Is your domestic church an expression of your Catholic faith? If not, how can you make it so?

What are some ways you demonstrate the importance of your family gathering together for dinner?

A PRAYER FOR THE JOURNEY

Dear Lord, please bless my domestic church from top to bottom. Remind us all each day to look to you and to do whatever it takes to help one another get closer to heaven. Dear Mother Mary, please inspire me each day to lead my family to your Son. Amen.

CHAPTER THREE

A Mother's Never-Ending Prayer

Rejoice in your hope, be patient in tribulation, be
constant in prayer.

—Romans 12:12

WHEN I TAKE MY DOG Sweetpea for a walk, I seldom take her all the
way down the driveway and then left out onto our private road.
Instead, I usually cut across the lawn so I can get out to the road
quicker to enjoy a bit of exercise, beautiful scenery, and fresh air
together. I've always felt that the shortest distance between two
points is a straight line. But when it comes to our prayer lives, we
can't take shortcuts.

As eager as we may be to get to where we should be, in reality
the path ahead oftentimes is not straight or easy; it's usually a rather
bumpy, curvy one. As tempting as it may be, if we try to go around
the bumps by "cutting across," we may very well miss important

lessons or graces that await us. I believe that it's within the nitty-gritty details of our daily lives that we will be formed into the Christians we are meant to be. We must experience it all—both the effortless and the arduous.

Sometimes the bumps in the road are profound and set us back in pain. Other times little inconveniences endured with patience open up opportunities for grace for others as well as for ourselves. I'll share from my own life an example of a small "bump in the road."

One Thursday evening after teaching my religious education class, my car wouldn't start. It had worked fine up until that point, so I was stumped about what the problem could be. Turning the key several more times proved futile. I had to call for a tow truck and find a ride home. I made some phone calls, and since my ride wouldn't be there for a while, feeling a tad annoyed, I waited as patiently as I could in my cold car, saying a few prayers.

A woman from my parish happened to walk through the parking lot, saw me waiting, and approached me. I got out of my car to greet her. I explained my predicament and then, with a heavy heart, the woman went on to tell me about a serious situation she was enduring. I felt the Holy Spirit give me words of comfort for her, and I gave her a hug. After we prayed together, her face seemed transformed and her voice sounded more hopeful. Had I left for home when I finished up my class, I wouldn't have encountered that woman or learned of her difficulties. I believe that God had everything under control from the start.

In the book *Light of the World*, Pope Benedict XVI—in an interview with author Peter Seewald—described the spiritual life by saying, "It is not as if, to use an image, an extra floor were added on top of our ordinary existence. The point is rather that inward contact with God through, with, and in Christ really does open in us new possibilities and enlarge our heart and our spirit. Faith truly does give our life a further dimension."[1]

There's no doubt in my mind about the importance prayer plays in a mother's life. At times, though, you may feel anxious and think that you couldn't possibly possess a serious prayer life, since your role as a mother keeps you quite engaged with the care of your household and family. Many areas in a mother's daily life can cause her to be concerned that either she's praying too much and neglecting her kids and household in the process or she's not praying enough and possibly neglecting God. While we do need to be cognizant about developing a solid prayer life, let's not get carried away with crazy ideas about what we think God may expect of us. After all, isn't he the One who has placed us in the heart of our home? Let's stop our stressing and look at the whole picture rationally. Throughout this chapter we'll look at the ways we can pray as attentive mothers.

Making Our Lives a Prayer

We learn from Deuteronomy, "You shall seek the LORD, your God; and you shall indeed find him when you search after him with your whole heart and your whole soul" (Deuteronomy 4:29). My former spiritual director (now deceased), Servant of God Fr. John A. Hardon, s.j., once said, "All prayer, from the highest raptures of mysticism to the lowly fingering of the beads, is a conversation with the invisible world of God, his angels, and the saints."[2]

How exactly do we pray as mothers? Some Catholic mothers prefer to sit or kneel in a familiar place to say their daily prayers, perhaps in a prayer chair or a prayer corner. I believe that our first prayer of the day should happen right at our bedside or even while we are still in bed. When I open my eyes to a new day, the words "Good morning, Jesus, thank you for a new day!" come from my lips to greet my Lord. Afterward, I make sure I offer a morning offering before I dive into my day.

In a revelation to St. Mechtilde (d. 1298), Our Lord said:

> When you awake in the morning, let your first act be to salute My Heart, and to offer Me your own.... Whoever shall breathe a sigh toward Me from the bottom of his heart when he awakes in the morning and shall ask Me to work all his works in him throughout the day, will draw Me to him.... For never does a man breathe a sigh of longing aspiration toward Me without drawing Me nearer to him than I was before.

As crazy-busy as mornings can be for us as mothers, we have to make a point to pause and pray. I sincerely believe that the morning may be the most important time of the day for prayer, even if we stop to pray only for a few minutes and are mindful of the spiritual element of the seemingly mundane as well as the more profound moments of prayer. The morning is, after all, a time of waking up to a clean slate—the new day ahead is filled with possibilities and opportunities for grace. Most graces are found hidden in the ordinary, it's true. So, let's be sure to take the time to kneel by the side of our bed as soon as we wake up so we can offer the whole day ahead to our dear Lord Jesus, asking him to transform the mundane, ordinary, and challenging into beautiful graces. Pray the words of the morning offering or use your own simple expressions of love for God and petitions and offerings. I pray a variation of this classic morning-offering prayer:

O Jesus, through the Immaculate Heart of Mary, I offer you my prayers, works, joys, and sufferings of this day, in union with the Holy Sacrifice of the Mass throughout the world. I offer them for all the intentions of Your Sacred Heart: the salvation of souls, reparation for sin and the reunion of all Christians. I offer them for the intentions of our bishops and of all apostles of prayer, and in particular for those recommended by our Holy Father this month.

St. Thérèse of Lisieux wrote a morning offering:

O my God! I offer thee all my actions of this day for the intentions and for the glory of the Sacred Heart of Jesus. I desire to sanctify every beat of my heart, my every thought, my simplest works, by uniting them to its infinite merits; and I wish to make reparation for my sins by casting them into the furnace of its merciful love.

O my God! I ask of thee, for myself and for those whom I hold dear, the grace to fulfill perfectly thy holy will, to accept for love of thee the joys and sorrows of this passing life, so that we may one day be united together in heaven for all eternity. Amen.

My morning offering is more like this:

O, Jesus, through the Immaculate Heart of Mary and through your most Sacred Heart, in union with all of the sacrifices of the Mass said throughout the world today, I offer you all of my prayers, works, joys, and sufferings of this day in reparation for the sins committed against the Immaculate Heart of Mary, for my sins, and for the sins of the whole world.

I ask you to please watch over all of my children and my husband and keep them close to you, dear Jesus. Please take care of all of the people on my prayer list, and please help all the people who have asked for my prayers. Please help the poor, the sick, the suffering, the dying, the troubled, and the souls in purgatory. Please use me to help others this day to turn them toward you. Please, dear Lord, grant me the graces this day to spread your love and do your holy will.

Blessed Mother Mary, please watch over my family and protect us from all evil and danger. Bring us closer to your Son, Jesus. All the angels and saints, please pray for us. St. Joseph, please pray for us. St. Michael, please protect us. Dear Mother Teresa, pray for us. Blessed John Paul II, pray for us. Amen.

I then speak to Jesus and Mary about things close to my heart, the needs of the day for myself and my family, for those who have asked for my prayers, and so on. I also invoke the saints who are dear to me (some were my friends here on earth!), asking for their help and intercession.

By starting our day with prayer, we'll have begun on the right foot. Then, after we have strapped on our own "oxygen mask," we need to make sure each child has done the same—that he or she has said their morning prayers. With your little ones, you'll want to join them in their simple yet powerful prayer. With the older ones, you'll want to "oversee" their morning prayers by setting the example and also offering them reminders, just as you would when instructing them to pick up after themselves or to take their vitamins and brush their teeth. "Have you said your prayers, honey? Did you say 'Good morning' to Jesus today?"

You can join in prayer with your husband before he rushes off to work, either in the bedroom, at the breakfast table, or even over the phone, as I do with my husband on many rushed mornings. Ideally, morning prayers said together as a family are best. When that is not possible, being sure that everyone has individually taken time to say his or her prayers is essential.

So, as the mom, the center of that hub of activity we call the family, your job regarding prayer is threefold: Establish a rich prayer life for yourself, teach your children to develop their own individual prayer lives, and gather up everyone together to pray as a family. These are the three ways you set prayer in motion in your domestic church.

Bl. Teresa of Calcutta loved Cardinal Newman's "Radiating Christ" prayer very much. She prayed it every day and instructed her sisters to do the same. It is surely a prayer that will inspire our own hearts to allow Jesus to live in us and through us each day.

Radiating Christ

Dear Jesus, help me to spread your fragrance everywhere I go.
Flood my soul with your spirit and life.
Penetrate and possess my whole being so utterly
that all my life may only be a radiance of yours.
Shine through me and be so in me
that every soul I come in contact with may feel your presence in my soul.

Let them look up and see no longer me but only Jesus!

Stay with me and then I shall begin to shine as you shine,

so to shine as to be a light to others;

the light, O Jesus, will be all from you;

none of it will be mine:

It will be you shining on others through me.

Let me thus praise you in the way you love best:

by shining on those around me.

Let me preach you without preaching, not by words, but by my example,

by the catching force,

the sympathetic influence of what I do,

the evident fullness of the love my heart bears to you.[3]

What's next? Are you able to attend daily Mass by yourself or with your children? This is something extremely worthwhile to strive for. Even one extra Mass per week would be a great step in the right direction. There may be a noon Mass at your parish—perhaps you could meet your husband there. There are many seasons in a mother's life. When the children are very young, it may at times be impossible to get out of the house to attend daily Mass, because someone is sick, for example, or there's bad weather. But when you're together in your domestic church, you can say a few prayers together at various times throughout the day.

In the next chapter we'll discuss teaching our children to pray as well as instituting the family rosary and other devotions. But for now, in this chapter, let's concentrate on getting the "oxygen mask" of prayer strapped properly onto ourselves first. After your morning offering, you'll do your best to fit in your prayers in between (and during) your tasks. Offering your heart to God and asking for his help and blessings throughout the day brings the necessary strength and grace to carry on.

One of the most selfless and loving sentiments I have ever heard came from the lips of an innocent child. During one of our religious education classes, we were discussing heaven, hell, and purgatory, and one of my third-grade students raised her hand. I called on her and she told the class that if she saw her twin sister "falling down to hell," she would "reach out and grab her to save her!" She innocently thought that she could literally reach out and snatch her sister from the peril of the eternal fires of hell. I complimented her for her courage and love and went on to explain that while she couldn't actually "save" her that way, she could save her sister through her prayers, love, and example before it ever got to that point.

Isn't this what we do as mothers with our prayers? We try to save our families from falling into hell. I believe that mothers' prayers stretch into eternity. A mother doesn't stop praying for her children until they are all safe in heaven. So our prayers are endless and powerful too. Consider St. Monica, St. Augustine's mother, for instance. Because of her never-ending prayers for him, he not only converted from his sinful life, he went on to become a saint and doctor of the Church! I like to think that the bishop's words in answer to St. Monica's pleadings when she cried her heart out to him, begging for help for her wayward son, are words that are meant for all mothers. He told her that it was impossible for God to turn his ear from the pleas of a faithful, prayerful mother. We can all be comforted knowing that our own never-ending prayers will be heard too. If there was hope for St. Augustine, there is certainly hope for our kids.

Being Both Martha and Mary

Many women struggle with trying to discern whether they should be more like Martha or more like Mary (the famous sisters we read about in the Gospels) with respect to their housekeeping and their spiritual life. Mary decided to sit at Jesus' feet, engaging in conversation with those gathered around him after he arrived at the sisters' house for an evening meal. Martha was busy in the kitchen, preparing the meal for Jesus and probably a dozen or more of his followers too. Martha's stress had reached its limit after she hadn't received the help she expected from her sister Mary, and she stomped into the other room to have a few words with her Lord.

"Lord, do you not care that my sister has left me to do all the work by myself? Tell her then to help me."

To which Jesus answered, "Martha, Martha, you are worried and distracted by many things; there is need of only one thing. Mary has chosen the better part which will not be taken away from her" (Luke 10:38–42).

Now, who was right, Martha or Mary? Of course, we don't doubt Jesus, who tells us that Mary chose "the better part." I do believe, though, that we mothers need to be like both Martha and Mary in our mothering and prayer life. Sometimes we're more in a Mary mode while other times a Martha mode is appropriate. In the course of our daily routine, we will find ourselves at times prayerfully contemplating and at other times actively engaged in our family's life. Our entire life can become a prayer when it is devoted to our Lord.

A Call to Holiness in the Here and Now

"Holiness," Bl. Teresa of Calcutta said, "is not the luxury of a few, but a duty for us all."[4] Yes, that's right, even mothers! How can a mother structure her day to be more fruitful in each of these areas we just discussed regarding Martha and Mary? There's no real concrete or decisive answer to this question, since a mother's life is really not her own. She gives herself in service to her family, and this requires a kind of selfless flexibility so that she can be attentive to the needs of everyone. Being *on call* to the needs of the family means that most times there's no telling when a solid prayer time can be scheduled or when a scheduled time may be interrupted.

Mothers know all too well how various crises can come up at any point throughout the day. For instance, suddenly a little one spikes a fever, or the washing machine goes on the fritz and overflows all over the place, or the kids start fighting, or a phone call comes in from the school nurse to drop everything and pick up a sick child, or the dog vomits on the carpet just as the neighbor kids ring the doorbell, wanting to play. Sometimes, all of the above happens at once! I have no doubt that you thoroughly understand what I am saying and probably have experienced this kind of craziness yourself—on more than one occasion too, I'll bet!

When you offer your whole life to God through prayer, you can trust that he will take care of everything. Say, for instance, that you set aside a half hour to pray the rosary while your little one naps, but she wakes up early with a nightmare and needs you. Or, your older child calls or texts, needing your immediate advice about a critical matter. Your rosary may have seemed to be interrupted as you set down your beads to comfort your daughter or help your older son. But in reality, it's only a pause until you are able to take up the next decade.

The time spent lovingly caring for your child was your prayer while serving, just like Martha. Your scheduled prayer time became a Martha and Mary prayer! By offering your life to our Lord, your loving service to your family is transformed into a prayer of active service. There is a profound peace that comes from knowing that our lives are actually living prayers to God. When a mother surrenders her life totally over to God's holy will, her life can be so amazing—it can become "something beautiful for God," in Bl. Teresa's famous expression.

As a mother, you are required to live in the present moment with your many duties to your family. As much as you may want to get to an extra Mass or an hour of Eucharistic Adoration, you can't just drop your mothering and run off to church when you are needed in your domestic church in the here and now. This is sometimes a tough quandary for mothers. Our Lord wants you to be at peace in your mothering. Acknowledge that you are in the heart of your home to raise your family well. You don't have any reason to feel pangs of guilt for not being able to be in two places at once or to do more than you actually can.

Bl. Teresa of Calcutta said that it is far easier to serve a "dish of rice" to a starving person on the other side of the world than it is to serve that same dish to someone in our own home. Serving that person on the other side of the world may consist of writing out a check or even traveling to help the unfortunate. It's often a lot more difficult for us to show our love to those we are close to! Maybe it's a teenager who is acting up, a toddler who is running circles around you, or a spouse who is difficult or grouchy. We must look around and see if there is someone in our own homes who is lacking or in need. Love begins there. The difficulties endured in raising Christian families may cause some mothers to seek out something else, to want to spread their love elsewhere. And, because women have big hearts, we sometimes feel compelled to do more to help others out in the community. But as much as we may want to "run away" at times or simply wish to help others, we would be wrong to neglect our duties at home only to go out and join committees, even very good ones.

First, let's serve that "dish of rice" to our loved ones at home. Then, if God gives us a surplus of time and energy and we know that all is well at home, we can roll up our sleeves and go out to help others too. My point is that we need to pause and search our hearts to be sure we're taking proper care of those whom God has entrusted to us. Let's be sure to get our priorities straight. Our Lord will help us.

The irritable, the angst-ridden, and the contradictory—those family members that challenge us in some way actually help us get to heaven. Truly! We need to ask God for grace and an extra dose of faith, hope, and love to love the very people God wants us to serve that dish of rice to. We are called to love them to heaven! In the course of one day God gives us so many opportunities to act on grace, to love our family members, to be exemplary in our selfless service to them. Sometimes the little loving details seem, well, *little*.

However, I am convinced that when we pray throughout our little details of loving service, these acts of love are really huge in God's eyes. He works through them all and sanctifies them.

"If I Touch Even His Garments, I Shall Be Made Well"

In Mark 5:21–34 we learn about a couple of miracles. One involves a brave and faithful woman who wants to touch Jesus' clothing, hoping for a healing. She says, "If I touch even his garments, I shall be made well" (Mark 5:28). To set the backdrop for a better understanding of what occurred just before this event: Jesus has been casting out demons and healing many people. Because of this, a crowd has gathered. Many are not followers but are waiting to see what kind of miracle or signs and wonders Jesus will perform next. Jairus, who is also mentioned in this Bible passage, is the leader of the local synagogue and normally would have nothing to do with Jesus. But we can surmise that he must have run out of other options, because he actually throws himself at Jesus' feet, begging for Jesus to heal his daughter, who is at the point of death.

Jesus does perform a miracle in answer to Jairus's pleas. But before it takes place, Jesus first responds to the faith-filled woman who approaches him with a heart full of faith, trust, and a whole lot of hope, reaching out to touch the hem of his garment. We don't even know this woman's name, but we know our Lord's response: "Daughter, your faith has made you well; go in peace, and be healed of your disease" (Mark 5:34).

This woman's deep faith and strong hope gave her the courage to reach out and touch Jesus' garment. Originally she had wanted to keep things on the quiet side, accepting the miracle and then going on her way in gratitude. Instead, she came clean and told Jesus everything when he asked who had touched his cloak.

Let's ponder these two miracles for a few moments. Jairus said, "Please lay your hands on my daughter." The woman didn't ask Jesus directly but touched his cloak, expecting a miracle. Did Jairus have less faith than the woman, because he was previously an unbeliever? Did Jesus respond to the unnamed woman first because of her great faith?

Both hoped and trusted that Jesus would help them in their dire need. Our Lord took care of them both. We were all given the extraordinary gift of faith at baptism. During our lifetime, our faith will increase, along with the virtues of hope and love. We may also experience times where our faith seems challenged. We must pray for our faith to grow. Each day, we should ask for an increase in faith. During the first three Hail Marys of the rosary, we ask for an increase in all three theological virtues: faith, hope, and love. Let's make it a point to ask for more and more faith. We definitely need it, don't we?

Perhaps we are hesitant in our faith journeys—timid, doubtful, or even fearful. Maybe we can't seem to find our way to Jesus' cloak. Perhaps we are lacking in hope. This may not be surprising, given the climate of our darkened world. Our culture bombards women with an onslaught of mixed messages, demands, and expectations. It's no wonder many women struggle to find Jesus' cloak—or might not even know they should look for it.

During our own journeys throughout life, our Lord allows us to rub elbows with those who may not have faith, so that we can be an example of faith, hope, and love to them through our words and actions. He surely places us in interesting circumstances, and this helps our own faith to grow too. We'll talk about this in more detail throughout this book.

If you scan the pages of Scripture, you will see that women were close to Jesus; women learned from him, accepted his teaching, and followed him. How can we reach out and touch our Lord's cloak in faith and complete surrender to his will? We live in a different era, no doubt, but we have the benefit of our holy Mother Church to teach us and lead us closer and closer to Jesus.

What would we have done if we were in that crowd? I might venture to say that we are possibly even more privileged than the woman who reached out and touched Jesus' cloak. Yes, she had heard that Jesus was a miracle worker, and she was in his physical presence. But we have the benefit of more than two thousand years of Church teaching to help us seek him.

What are we praying and pondering as we approach Jesus in Holy Communion? Do we recognize that we too can *touch* his "cloak?" We can! Let's pray for that amazing awareness of the presence of Christ. We can recall Jesus' words when he brought Jairus's daughter back to life: "Do not fear, only believe" (Mark 5:36).

R E F L E C T I O N

What are some ways you can schedule "nothing" into your day so that opportunities are opened for your child to climb up on your lap, play a board game, engage in a meaningful conversation with an older child, or say some heartfelt prayers?

Do you place importance on your morning prayer, starting your day off on the right foot? If not, what might you do to create a new habit?

Do you serve a "dish of rice" to your family before committing to other endeavors? If you are sensing that some of your outside commitments might be getting in the way of this, what steps can you take to change it?

A PRAYER FOR THE JOURNEY

Dear Lord, help me to be open to the needs of my family in every way. Let me see clearly that my role is in getting them all to heaven through my example and love. Please grant me an increase in faith, hope, and love. Dear Mother Mary, please intercede for all of us as we work out our salvation. Amen.

CHAPTER FOUR

First and Foremost Educator

The right and the duty of parents to educate their children are primordial and inalienable.

—Bl. John Paul II

WHEN I WAS GROWING UP, I used to think that the idea that I later heard summed up in the adage "It takes a village to raise a child" was pretty accurate and even kind of idyllic. After all, we seem to become a product of our environment, so wouldn't it be ideal to have all that help in raising our young? Now, as a mother of five on earth and three in heaven, I recognize that a faithful Catholic mother should never want her "village" (society or the government) to raise her child, at least not in this day and age! We know all too well what is happening around us in our world, much of it precisely what we want to keep our children away from. Our culture doesn't share our values—we don't want to set our kids free on the streets of New York City any time soon, or even in the woods where I live in New England. The closely knit community in Africa where this familiar proverb evidently originated is not necessarily similar to what we experience in our own neighborhoods—and certainly not in the larger culture.

As idyllic as the phrase sounds, mothers need to be very careful when it comes to entrusting the care of their children to others. We mustn't be naïve. Just think of what could have happened if Mary and Joseph had allowed the village to raise Jesus.

The Church teaches us:

> Since parents have conferred life on their children, they have a most solemn obligation to educate their offspring. Hence, parents must be acknowledged as the first and foremost educators of their children. Their role as educators is so decisive that scarcely anything can compensate for their failure in it. For it devolves on parents to create a family atmosphere so animated with love and reverence for God and others that a well-rounded personal and social development will be fostered among children. Hence, the family is the first school of those social virtues which every society needs.[1]

Parents certainly have a high calling, so let's be extra mindful of our sublime and sacred responsibilities. We also learn from *Gravissimum Educationis* that "the *role of parents in education* is of such importance that it is almost impossible to provide an adequate substitute."[2] The *Catechism* tells us that "parents have the first responsibility for the education of their children. They bear witness to this responsibility first by *creating a home* where tenderness, forgiveness, respect, fidelity, and disinterested service are the rule. The home is well suited for *education in the virtues*. This requires an apprenticeship in self-denial, sound judgment, and self-mastery— the preconditions of all true freedom. Parents should teach their children to subordinate the 'material and instinctual dimensions to interior and spiritual ones.'"[3] These are words to keep in mind as we are raising our children. We will ultimately answer to God about how our children have been educated. We are, after all, their "first and foremost educator."

"Don't Put That Garbage in Your Head!"

Educating our children properly and protecting them from the lurking dangers in our culture requires that we have a handle on our own view of the world and on what we allow ourselves to be exposed to. Just because we are the adults, this does not mean we are immune to temptation or that we can handle all of the images presented to us by the culture through the media, the Internet, video games, music, television, and advertising.

My dear friend Fr. Bill C. Smith (now deceased) used to warn our congregation, "Don't put that garbage in your head!" He was referring to inappropriate movies, images, and television shows. He cautioned us that whatever goes into our minds will stay there, as much as we wish it wouldn't. And "you know who" (as I call the evil one) uses that garbage we've put into our minds to try and trip us up and cause us to fall, typically at the most inopportune moments.

Servant of God Rev. John A. Hardon, s.j., preached about the "custody of the senses." In his book *Modern Catholic Dictionary*, he describes "custody of the senses" like this: "In Christian asceticism, the practice of controlling the use of the senses, especially the eyes, in order to foster union with God and preserve oneself in virtue. It is founded on the premise that 'nothing is in the mind that was not first in the senses.' Sense experience inevitably produces thoughts in the mind; thoughts become desires; and desires lead to actions. Morally good actions, therefore, ultimately depend on a judicious guard of sensations."[4]

How do we guard our senses—especially in today's world, where we are bombarded with images through advertising and the media, when just about anything is acceptable and most of it draws us away from God? Here are some guidelines for avoiding use of our senses in ways that would lead us away from God and for using them instead to lead us closer to him:

Sense of sight: Avoid viewing images that are impure or indecent in movies, television, pictures, magazines, websites, games, and everyday life. For example, if you see someone dressed immodestly, turn your eyes away from him or her. If you are talking with the person, maintain eye contact and avoid looking at their body.

Sense of hearing: Don't listen to impure or indecent music and media. Always avoid listening to gossip. Make time for silence and prayer so you can listen to God. To do this, avoid too much television, radio, Internet, and idle chatter.

Sense of taste: Don't eat or drink to excess—this is considered gluttony.

Sense of touch: Avoid any occasion of sinful touch. Any touch that is sensual or sexual and does not fall within the bounds of a Christian marriage is sinful.

In addition to teaching this almost lost "conscience guide" to our children, we want to heed the same rules ourselves. We must keep in mind that our actions will always speak much louder than our words, especially with our kids! For instance, I am surprised at how many people watch idiotic television shows. It would seem they have nothing else to keep their interest, which is sad. Some of the popular primetime shows are downright offensive and exploitative toward women and often disparaging toward men as well. Let's be sure that our habits aren't stumbling blocks to our own growth in holiness or to our children as we teach them how to avoid the "near occasion of sin," another phrase we would be wise to keep alive in our world today.

A "near occasion of sin" simply means, according to the *Modern Catholic Dictionary*, "any person, place, or thing that of its nature or because of human frailty can lead one to do wrong, thereby committing sin."[5] Pornography, for example, is always a near occasion of sin. A situation, person, or thing may be a "near occasion of sin" to one person and not another. Through past experiences or just plain common sense, we usually have a pretty good idea of those situations, persons, and things in life that, when encountered, may cause us to fall into sin. These are what we must avoid and what we should teach our children to avoid too. We should never put ourselves in harm's way by throwing caution to the wind with a lackadaisical or naïve attitude. There may indeed be grave consequences for doing so. If we are unsure of what might be a "near occasion of sin" for us, we should seek spiritual counsel to learn more about it so we can better guide our children and stay away from the dangers and temptations ourselves. Taking time to contemplate the Ten Commandments will help us as well.

A recent article stated that one-third of women aged eighteen through thirty-four check their Facebook accounts before doing anything else in the morning, including going to the bathroom—some even get up in the middle of the night to do so.[6] Perhaps the over-age-thirty-four crowd (not mentioned in the article) might possibly go to the bathroom first and then run to their computers or cell phones! I'm only half-joking—women of all ages are becoming addicted to social media and sometimes might identify with it more than with real life!

Our first priority should be to get on our knees first thing in the morning to thank God for the blessing of a new day and to ask his help for us to get through it with grace. We've become way too obsessed with getting connected in cyberspace via the Internet and social networking and much less concerned about our relationship with God and the people around us. Mothers, be aware of how your example impacts your children! Checking Facebook or e-mail and surfing the Internet before starting our day with prayer and engaging in real-life encounters and conversations with our families has definite consequences—not only for us but for our families as well.

Forging a United Front

When it comes to parenting our children in a holy manner, spouses must work together. Many studies have shown that one of the biggest complaints spouses have (besides disagreeing about finances) is about how to raise their kids. Parents must forge a united front in raising their children. This requires honest communication with your spouse. And it's a good idea to think about how to raise them *before* you have them! Granted, some things are "in the moment" kinds of teachings, but it's essential to take the time and discuss mutual goals and ideals during your courtship. However, for those who haven't discussed their parenting strategies and Christian values, it is never too late—or perhaps I should say "better late than never." Open the doors of communication now. If you are a single mother or if your husband doesn't share your concerns about raising your children on the straight and narrow, you are responsible for that teaching. We'll talk about that in more depth later on.

The graces from the sacrament of marriage give us strength and courage to teach our children in the best way possible. Remember to call on these graces through prayer each day, even when you are weary, even if you feel a bit hopeless. We are fueled additionally through the sacramental life of the Church by receiving the Eucharist and frequenting the confessional. This enables us to be equipped to handle all matters, come what may.

If you discover that your children's school is teaching error (even if it's a Catholic school!), you can seek to remedy the situation. If that's not possible, don't hesitate—take them out. If your children are hanging out with the wrong crowd, do all you can to steer them away. If you know that trash and filth are coming into your home through cable TV, get rid of the cable box. Most television shows today are doing nothing more than selling sex along with an "anything goes" attitude. Perhaps I might seem a little dramatic, but if we don't protect our children, who will? The village? We have to be proactive, vigilant, and totally wide awake and aware in all areas of child rearing.

Interestingly, after beginning this chapter, I came across a statement expressed on a bumper sticker. It said, "I homeschool because I have seen the village and I don't want it raising my children." Not all mothers are able to homeschool their children for one reason or another, but it is a very effective educational choice, and it is becoming more and more popular with concerned parents.

In the mid-1970s, Archbishop (and now Servant of God) Fulton Sheen said that if we want our children to fight for their faith, we should send them to public school, and that if we want them to lose their faith, we should send them to Catholic school. He was a man who did not mince words, and he lamented the errors being taught in many Catholic schools. At the time, homeschooling was not an option in most areas. It's just as necessary, if not more so, today to investigate the curriculum in our children's schools (whether private or public) before making decisions about their education. It's a grave responsibility—one that parents should take seriously.

Teaching Our Children to Be Prayerful

The very best way to teach your children to be prayerful is to set an example of prayer right from the start. I remember being in a quiet church by myself one day, praying before the Blessed Sacrament. Suddenly, I heard the sounds of children running into the church. Apparently their mother had brought them there so they could light candles and pray, most likely for a special intention. As the children exuberantly made their way to the candles, the mom was shushing them, no doubt fearful of disturbing me. But the sounds didn't bother me at all. Rather, they warmed my heart, knowing that a beautiful tradition was being set for those children.

It is indeed a high priority for us as parents to guide our children in their religious education through programs they attend at church or school as well as through our instruction at home. It's up to us to make sure they participate regularly at Mass and partake of the sacraments and help them develop and nurture an invaluable habit of prayer that will take them through life.

To do this, we can start as early as possible to set an example of prayer in the home. In addition to making your home a sacred and comforting dwelling for your family, you can teach your children that praying is as natural as eating. It's at the heart of our lives as Catholics and it's an amazing treasure and comfort. Communicate to your children that prayer is their personal conversation with God and that he loves to hear from them anytime. They should never fear approaching him.

Being Aware of the Culture's Pressures and Influence

Parents need to keep their eyes on the culture to understand the influence it has on their children. For instance, let's look at cell-phone and Internet use. Young children owning cell phones has become the norm rather than the exception in modern suburbia. Many parents have admitted to me that they have caved in over the cell-phone issue. Basically, their children pressured them so much that they finally gave in. It's so acceptable for kids to have cell phones these days that parents may not recognize the dangers initially.

Regarding technology, is it important for our kids to be in constant contact with their friends? No. Personally, I don't believe children under the age of sixteen should have cell phones. Even at sixteen, we must still be vigilant in protecting them, and not every sixteen-year-old is mature enough to own one. It opens them up to a whole world of texting and to being in touch with people without your knowledge as well as to being exposed to the Internet without filters or parental control. Even if their phones don't have the capability of accessing the Internet, texting and phone calling are areas where kids shouldn't be navigating unsupervised. Of course, it's another story if your child is of babysitting or employment age and needs a cell phone in case of emergencies.

Before the ability to access the Internet via cell phones, parents needed to be concerned only with monitoring the use of computers in their homes. But now the home computer is not the only culprit in pornography use or exposure, it's the cell phone too. Children are being exposed to this horrible epidemic in America at much earlier ages. Studies have shown that many children are first exposed to pornography by age eleven, and in some instances even earlier. Perhaps this may be too shocking to believe, but studies show that a total of 90 percent of children ages eight to sixteen have viewed online pornography.[7] Exposure to pornography leads to the death of innocence and is truly a desecration of all that is holy and sacred.

Another dark area we want our children to avoid is "sexting." According to an online CBS News article, "The practice of 'sexting'—sending nude pictures via text message—is not unusual, especially for high schoolers around the country."[8] Even if you think there's no way your young teen would ever participate in sexting, they may still be exposed to it, because these images are often shared with others not meant to see them initially. Approximately 20 percent of teens admit to having participated in sexting, according to a survey by the National Campaign to Support Teen and Unplanned Pregnancy. [9]

This same agency offers tips for how parents can set expectations with their children. One tip is:

> Make sure you are clear with your teen about what you consider appropriate "electronic" behavior. Just as certain clothing is probably off-limits or certain language unacceptable in your house, make sure you let your kids know what is and is not allowed online either. And give reminders of those expectations from time to time. It doesn't mean you don't trust your kids, it just reinforces that you care about them enough to be paying attention. [10]

The issues surrounding children and cell phones require serious parental consideration. Other electronic devices and forms of media can fall into the questionable and dangerous category as well. In addition to the potential dangers is the temptation for children to be constantly connected.

Kids these days are so accustomed to instant everything. The world can become nothing more than a bunch of sound bites, text messages, or one-line status updates for our youth and young adults. Where have the real human encounters gone? As this book is being printed, many new forms of technology and social communication are being developed. We live in a fast-paced media world, after all. There is much that is positive in advancing technologies, and Bl. John Paul II and Pope Benedict XVI have even encouraged use of new media for evangelization. However, we as parents must strenuously protect our children from the negative, unhealthy, and, yes, evil aspects of it.

A young teen was visiting our home. Trying to divert her from her constant use of technology, I asked her why she was so eager to know our wireless password, which would enable her to connect to the Internet with her iPod Touch. She told me that she wanted to contact a friend. To make my point a bit dramatically, I showed her our telephone, sweeping my arms in its direction, much like Vanna White from *Wheel of Fortune*. This young lady didn't miss a beat; she said, "Oh, no, I don't use the phone—I *text*." I suggested that she and her friend might enjoy a phone conversation together. That went over like a lead balloon. I didn't give in, though. I think it almost killed her, but she managed to get through the visit at our home without access to the Internet for a few short hours. No doubt, she sent a text the first chance she had after she left.

We must be aware of what is offered to teens and tweens via the television and cable. "By some estimates," according to the *New York Times*, "half of American children have a television in their bedroom; one study of third graders put the number at 70 percent. And a growing body of research shows strong associations between TV in the bedroom and numerous health and educational problems."[11] Many shows targeted to this age group, particularly on the MTV channel, promote sex, drugs, and other unethical, immoral, and unacceptable behavior. Years ago, I paid extra to have my cable company remove MTV from my plan. I trusted my children not to watch it and other ungodly shows, but I refused to allow even the possibility of that filth coming into my domestic church. It takes time and effort, but we can find good media for our children to enjoy in place of the bad stuff.

So that your children are not on the Internet unnecessarily, set firm, clear boundaries regarding its use as well as the use of cell phones and mp3 players. Place the computer in a family area, not in a child's bedroom. Allowing children to roam the Internet without you is like letting them loose in a world of strangers without supervision—or even worse, openly inviting into your home questionable characters along with the destruction they bring with them.

You, like many parents, might not be aware that your kids have multiple identities on social networking sites. You may think you are safely monitoring them, and they've outsmarted you! What is a parent to do? Be more vigilant and don't be stupid! As Jesus tells us, "Be shrewd as serpents and simple as doves" (Matthew 10:16, *NAB*). We must develop a stronger backbone—we can't be afraid to say No to our kids. If we are not strong and protective, our kids may be subjected to slander, bullying, pornography, and, via the Internet, other dangers that in some cases can lead to depression and suicidal thoughts or actions. Sit down with them and talk with them.

Because parents have allowed children to have too much freedom with respect to the Internet, texting, television, and social media, we're beginning to see a generation of kids going down the tubes. We are stewards of our children; they are on loan to us from God. We must take our responsibilities seriously.

Too much time with today's technology takes your children away from the family, where they ought to be interacting in the flesh, not via cyberspace. An excessive use of social utilities ties up valuable time that could have been used for exercise, taking care of one's hygiene, time out in the fresh air, just thinking their own thoughts, or time for God through family prayer or personal prayer, education, or reading. Perhaps it's about time to pare down on technology for the betterment of the children and the family as a whole.

Stanford communications professor Clifford Nass, quoted in a *New York Times* article online, said that the overuse of technology diminishes empathy by limiting how much people engage with one another even when they are in the same room. He said, "The way we become more human is by paying attention to each other.... It shows how much you care." Nass says that empathy is essential to the human condition and that "a significant fraction of people's experiences are now fragmented" because of the overuse of technology.[12]

Archbishop Charles Chaput of Philadelphia expressed grief about another area where the culture has failed our youth. Addressing an audience attending "Faith in the Public Square," a conference in British Columbia, he said that youth today are suffering because Catholics have failed to transmit the faith to the next generation. As a result, young people have lost their "moral vocabulary." Specifically he said, "Our culture is doing catechesis every day. It works like water dripping on a stone, eroding people's moral and religious sensibilities, and leaving a hole where their convictions used to be."[13]

Wow! We have to wake up and find out what's going on around us! I point this out not to cause feelings of hopelessness or despair but to spark a greater sense of responsibility in Catholic parents. If Christian parents do not properly pass down the faith to their children and aren't careful to shield them from the dangers of the culture, they are allowing the culture to leave a large hole in their children's souls. In later chapters we'll discuss some of the societal demands of our culture.

Our Grown Children

Our grown children, who were once itty-bitty babies in our arms, so utterly permeating our world, are now full-size adults making lives of their own. How did that happen so fast? Going off to college or, afterward, into marriage, they are bid loving "good-byes" by their parents. However, it's never really "good-bye"—rather, "see you soon!" Or, at least that's what mothers hope for.

I firmly believe that once a mother, always a mother, no matter how old our children become. We will mother them much differently when they are older, of course. Naturally, when our children become adults, they are free to make their own choices and are no longer under our authority. As their mother, we can still influence and guide them with our example, and we can certainly pray for them, even into eternity. A mother's prayers are powerful, and it's good to recall this truth, especially at times when it may not seem so. We can trust in the power of prayer and God's love for our families.

Let us hope your grown children are faring well in the great big world. There's a very special peace and a feeling of accomplishment that a parent experiences on seeing her grown children making their way in the world and staying true to their upbringing. Some grown children may not be doing as well. How do we love them, even in their sin? I've known parents who would not attend their son's or daughter's wedding because they had lived with their spouse before marriage. How must that feel to a son or daughter, knowing that their own parent wouldn't attend their wedding? How will that affect the future when grandchildren come into the world?

There are parents who won't welcome a daughter back home because she had an abortion. While an abortion is a horrendous crime in the eyes of the Church, are we above God, who is all-merciful? Sons and daughters are turned away also because they have left the Church. Some are kicked out of the home under the premise of "tough love." While there is such a thing as "tough love" for some situations, I don't believe that parents should render judgment through the way they treat their grown children. What will that teach them about Christianity? It's always better to err on the side of love in all dealings with our children.

Perhaps it might seem to take an inordinate amount of trust for us to believe that God actually loves our children even more than we do. Too often, parents "hit" their grown children over the head with judgment and their own beliefs instead of loving them and in that way patiently guiding them. We might be required to keep on loving them, despite everything. More love, less lecture. Living our faith speaks volumes.

Before talking with your grown children, invoke your guardian angel as well as theirs to help you and them. Ask the Holy Spirit to guide your conversations.

R E F L E C T I O N

Are your eyes open to the dangers your children face from the culture? What areas do you need to be more aware of?

Do you fully realize your grave responsibilities in raising your children in the truth of the faith? List these responsibilities in order of importance, and make them a matter of prayer.

What ways have you risked being unpopular with your kids in your effort to ensure they are safely on the straight and narrow path that leads to heaven? How can you be more vigilant with respect to lurking dangers?

A PRAYER FOR THE JOURNEY

Dear Lord, grant me the strength, courage, and wisdom that I need each day to guard, protect, and guide my family closer to you. Dear Mother Mary, protect us from the snares of the devil and shower your graces upon my family. Amen.

Mothering Our
Daughters and Sons

To maintain a joyful family requires much from both the
parents and the children. Each member of the family has
to become, in a special way, the servant of the others.

—Bl. John Paul II

OVER THE YEARS I HAVE heard many parents express that they prefer
boys over girls or vice versa. Personally, I don't know how anyone
can choose one over another. Both daughters and sons are blessings
beyond what we deserve, but as we raise them, it's wise to keep in
mind that there are differences between the sexes. I am blessed to
have three daughters and two sons, so I have been given the gift of
parenting both sexes.

Growing up with five brothers gave me a good dose of boy stuff.
My two sisters were influential too, but because they were much
older I was mostly surrounded by my brothers. I climbed trees,
built forts, dug up worms for fishing, caught toads, and played

cowboys and Indians. If I wasn't playing with my dolls, cats, and stuffed animals, daydreaming about horses, drawing, or reading, I was hanging with my brothers. I think it made me well-rounded, and I'm glad to have had these experiences. My mother didn't shy away from dressing me up in pretty dresses and hair ribbons, though, when I wasn't in my tomboy attire. As often as she could steal me from making mud pies, she took me under her wing to show me around the kitchen. She assigned me the jobs of setting the table and drying the dishes and always lovingly reminded me that I was a girl.

Mothering Our Daughters

Pretty hair bows, dolls, playing house, having tea parties, and doing all kinds of girly, frilly things—right from the start, that's what our little girls' lives are filled with, right?

Yet, all too soon, they toss their dolls aside for makeup and fashion and suddenly become interested in dating boys. They grow up so fast these days. Is it possible to slow time down a bit so they can enjoy their childhood? That may be a nearly impossible feat at a time when young girls are presented with such alluring, provocative, and confusing messages by today's culture. Still, our goal is to help our daughters to enjoy their childhoods in a healthy and wholesome way. It is possible to preserve their beautiful younger years. We can encourage femininity in our daughters and help them to recognize their special feminine gifts from God—receptivity, sensitivity, generosity, and maternity, to name just a few.

I overheard the young mother sitting in the chair next to me at the hair salon tell her stylist that her young teenage daughter still enjoyed playing with her dolls at home but didn't want her friends to know about it. Turns out, her daughter Sophie has "secret" dolls. In fact, Sophie will carefully hide all her dolls if her girlfriends are coming over for a visit, and she explicitly tells her younger siblings each time to keep her dolls a secret. It's too bad that a young girl feels she has to hide her childhood.

Let's take a look at the dolls available for our daughters. We may naïvely think the fashion dolls that are all the rage today are innocuous, but let's take a closer look. According to an article in *MSN Health and Fitness*, "It's not just pop stars who are to blame for popularizing looks that are too sexy for grammar school. The latest culprit in this culture war is something seemingly innocent—a line of dolls." The writer is speaking of the Bratz® dolls, which, she reports, are marketed "as dolls with 'a passion for fashion.'" She notes that the fashions include "low-cut jeans and halter tops worn over little, girl-like bodies." She adds that the company that produces them, MGA Entertainment, "says the dolls are geared toward girls ages seven to eleven, but girls as young as four are eager to play with them too. And in a culture that glorifies fashion, runway models, and celebrity cover girls, it's no surprise that the obsession would trickle down even to preschool fashionistas."[1]

Susan Linn, cofounder of the Campaign for a Commercial-Free Childhood (CCFC), believes that "little girls are being encouraged to immerse themselves in the preoccupations of adolescence." "They are going straight from preschool to teenager," she cautions, "and skipping over the important development stages that should take place during middle childhood." Parents need to take notice. Linn believes that "the [Bratz] dolls encourage girls to think about themselves as sexualized objects whose power is equated with dressing provocatively."[2]

Diane Levin, a professor in the early-education department at Wheelock College in Boston, said that

> at a time in their development when children are trying to understand what it means to be a boy or a girl, they are getting the narrowest possible image of what those gender roles mean. If what girls are learning as early as preschool is that they have to be sexy and attractive, that is supposedly setting them up for self-image issues and eating disorders later on.[3]

The next time you reach for a doll or toy at the toy store, be sure to pause and consider its suggestion and message.

Recently at the grocery store I bumped into Lynn, a woman I hadn't seen for a while. Her children were former students in a preschool program I used to run. After exchanging hugs, Lynn leaned over to whisper in my ear. What she had to say was too delicate to be uttered aloud.

"I can't believe it," she whispered. "They told Emma all about boys and their 'wet dreams.'" She sighed and looked at me as if defeated. Lynn was referring to the required sex-education course being taught at her daughter's public school. Lynn had opted to keep her daughter in the class because she didn't want her to feel like the odd one out, but she was very upset and felt her nine-year-old was much too young to be hearing this kind of thing. Are you really aware of what information and images your kids are being subjected to—even at school?

It's not so simple to mother our daughters these days. Just when we think we've figured out how old is old enough for them to wear makeup, we are faced with whether or not we should listen to our pediatrician who tells us our daughters need the HPV vaccination (licensed as Gardasil or Cervarix). What is the Church's stance on this popular vaccine? The Church teaches that the decision to vaccinate against HPV must be made by the parent.

I turned to a board-certified pediatrician friend, Dr. Tessa V. Perez, who said that "for parents making the decision whether to vaccine against HPV, it's really not complicated when you consider that it is a vaccine for a sexually transmitted disease. Human papilloma virus [HPV] can be transmitted only with sexual contact."

There's a lot of pressure to have young girls vaccinated against HPV. Parents are told that the HPV vaccine will protect their daughter from cervical cancer. While this is partially true, it is important to know that the vaccines are not cancer vaccines. Both vaccines protect against infection with HPV types 16 and 18, which can cause about 70 percent of cervical cancers. Gardasil additionally protects against type 6 and 11. The duration of immunity is not known at this time. Some studies show that protection lasts only about four years, which means boosters may be required in the future. More research is still necessary. Also, it's important to know that there are many other types of HPV that can cause infection leading to cervical cancer. The recommendation for pap tests is still essential to detect cancer or precancerous changes. Dr. Perez reminds us that "the message a parent sends a child when they tell them to wait for marriage to engage in sexual intercourse but then give them this vaccine is, 'OK, I've told you why you should wait, but I'm giving you this shot because I don't believe you can do it.'" I agree with her—parents clearly send their daughters a contradictory message when agreeing to vaccinate them. Dr. Perez recommends that we provide our children with the necessary knowledge by "first explaining to them the Catholic teaching on chastity and then later letting them know the reality of fornication, which can include pregnancy, STDs, and infertility." We should indeed, Dr. Perez points out, explain the consequences of sexual behavior to our children, but that should not be the main reason we are instructing them to avoid premarital sex. "As parents," she explains, "we have to help our children understand the beauty and holiness of the marital union, so that they see why the good of this union can be completely experienced only when it is sacramental. The best method I know is Pope John Paul's beautiful Theology of the Body." The Gardasil vaccine is also now being given to boys. The FDA approved Gardasil for use in males ages nine to twenty-six to prevent genital warts caused by HPV 6 and HPV 11. By the time you are reading this book, there may be other similar vaccinations that you need to investigate. The key here is that we cannot just simply accept what the world considers necessary for our children.[4]

Modesty, Fashion, and Makeup

"The dress of the body should not discredit the good of the soul," St. Cyprian of Carthage (AD 200–258) observed as long ago as the third century. Today, however, virtually anything goes in our current culture. So much is accepted: premarital sex, promiscuity, same-sex attractions (which are encouraged and included in present-day school curricula), and the list goes on, much to our dismay.

When a woman and her eleven-year-old daughter came to visit me one day, I was totally taken aback by the young girl's appearance. I'm sorry to say that she looked like a prostitute. She was wearing extremely short shorts and a skintight, low-cut, revealing tank top, and she sported provocative coal-black eyeliner, drawn around her eyes in very thick lines that added years to her face. Her mom apparently accepted her daughter's fashion statement. I asked myself why this seemingly innocent tween felt a need to dress beyond her years—and in an inappropriate way too. I was even more curious about why her mother thought her daughter's attire was acceptable. The young girl might have felt it was cool to dress this way, or maybe it made her feel "pretty." Did she have any idea what type of attention she might attract by dressing in this manner?

Unfortunately, many parents today just go with the flow of the culture. There's no way to mince words: They lack a moral backbone. Some choose not to make waves, wanting to be a popular parent. Being a good parent doesn't mean you will always be all the rage with your children. It's a serious responsibility to protect our children from the dangers that lurk in an ungodly world. It's up to us to teach them how they should present themselves—always with modesty and dignity and never in an alluring, provocative, or sexy way. Yet, just about every ad or article in teen magazines or on television tells them otherwise. In many cases, in the child's eyes, the parent becomes the oddball, the "old-fashioned" one who doesn't have a clue about what's cool and what's in with today's fashion. But in reality, spiritually aware parents are very much in tune with the culture, and because they are, they are more equipped to protect their children from its dangers.

It's not an easy task to keep a tight rein on fashion choices for your kids because of what they observe from their peers, babysitters, neighbors, and mass media. People wear immodest clothing even to Mass. Do these women and girls realize what they are revealing to everyone each time they bend over? We are not meant to see their bare breasts, their upper thighs, their derriere, or their underwear! Do they ever consider that they may be a stumbling block to others?

After Mass one Sunday, I observed a mother wearing a very low-cut blouse (accompanied by her daughter who was wearing a micro-mini) go up and give our pastor a big hug. I could only imagine what might have gone through his mind to see both mother and daughter clad so immodestly in God's house!

It is times like that when I wish I could gently wrap a beautiful shawl around each of the tweens and teens I see wearing low-cut or skintight clothing. I wish I could tell them that showing off their bodies will get them the wrong kind of attention, that their bodies are precious and should not be shown off in that way. I wish I could let them know that, by giving into the demands of an ungodly culture, they are buying into an exploitation of who they are. At every turn the world bombards them with the idea that dressing provocatively is very fashionable and makes them look "gorgeous." The goal should be fashionably modest, not sexy.

"It is very hard to find suitable clothes for a little girl," Josie, a Catholic mother of four, laments, "because the clothes the stores offer are aimed at dressing them not just like they are older but like older girls who have no respect for their bodies." I understand her sentiments; I often feel frustrated about the lack of appropriate feminine clothing available for *me!* It seems that predominantly sexy and immodest clothing is what's available. In fact, I had to be creative and wear a matching camisole under the dress I wore to my son's wedding. Even though the dress I chose didn't have a plunging neckline, I was not comfortable knowing that it would be slightly revealing.

Women young and old need to stand their ground about their feminine dignity and dress modestly. This can indeed set an example for others to follow. I'm tempted to start my own clothing company! When we dress modestly we are in essence saying, "I respect myself, and I respect you too."

I believe that some of the inappropriate fashion choices that are so prevalent today stem from the fact that so many girls and women are starved for love and attention. They may be searching for it in all the wrong places, innocently believing that showing off their bodies will make them more likeable or desirable in some way. I wonder if their fathers have given them enough fatherly love and affection.

Along these same lines, do you encourage your husband to express to your daughter that she is beautiful in so many ways? Is she complimented about her many God-given gifts and talents, her spirit, her mind, heart, and soul? You don't want her to run off later on in life with the first guy who tells her she's pretty or to feel the need to show off in some way to attract attention from the opposite sex. Affirmation from a father (or a father figure) early in life helps a daughter not only to feel loved but to experience more self-respect and self-confidence.

I chose to elaborate on some aspects of the degrading, immodest fashions prevalent today because I believe they exploit and hurt women and girls. No doubt there are many other fashion statements that we'll need to address in order to discern whether or not it's an expression of identity or something that is harmful for our daughters.

Daughters are such treasures! Each one brings amazing blessings to our lives despite any tough times we may be required to endure in raising them. I have thoroughly enjoyed mothering each of my daughters—they have kept me on my toes and continue to give me zillions of reasons to thank God for them in my life.

Mothering Our Sons

Trucks, tractors, airplanes, sports games, rough-and-tumble play, and little-boy treasures—it's what fills a boy's life right from the start, right? Our sons bring such joyful energy to our lives!

I can remember feeling so left out when I couldn't go on a fishing trip with my father and older brothers—just because I was a little girl! That didn't sit right with me; I had a craving for adventure too. But, unbeknownst to me at that time, the real reason was that my father didn't know how he could handle the needs of a seven-year-old girl requiring a bathroom when on a motorboat miles and miles out on Long Island Sound!

As I reminisce about when my first child, Justin, was born, an incident comes to mind. A friend visited me at the hospital and commented on his beautiful cherub face and quickly added that Justin would be shaving that face one day.

What? My mind couldn't begin to imagine whiskers on that porcelain-looking newborn face all of a few days old. Why do people want to rush babies to grow up? My little boy had plenty of time for that. I would be content to have him in my arms for as long as possible, I thought.

Later on, when Justin was a young boy in school, I told him not to fight back on the playground when other little boys were picking fights and causing trouble. I wanted him to walk away from it, to be a little "Jesus," I suppose. Sr. Frances, who was on recess duty at my son's Catholic school, told me that he needed to have my permission to fight back. She taught me that there is indeed a difference between self-defense and fighting, and she helped me to see that Justin should be allowed to protect himself if he was put in a bad position. It's something we need to think about, even though we want our children to avoid fighting whenever possible and to set a shining Christian example of peace and justice.

Parents need to instill and encourage masculine characteristics in our sons. We need to help them recognize that God has given them special masculine gifts with which to serve him and the good of others—our sons' courage and strength as protector and provider will unfold and grow with our support.

When my son Joseph defended his college friend from a vicious gang one evening in the Bronx by pushing one brute off his buddy, I was extremely upset about the whole ordeal, but I thanked God on my knees that Joseph wasn't killed. I was also proud of him for using his masculine gifts to bring justice.

Amy, a Catholic mother of four sons and five daughters, told me she doesn't believe the pop psychologists who "tell us little girls and little boys are born exactly the same." Amy believes that boys and girls are "definitely born with certain characteristics that separate them from each other as boys and girls." I wholeheartedly agree. Amy parents in a way to foster femininity in her girls and masculinity in her boys, which she feels is "especially important in today's culture where being 'equal' means making boys into girls and girls into boys."

"A house full of boys can be a noisy place!" Amy observed. She believes that boys are born active. "As soon as my boys can crawl, they try to take apart the computer or remote control. They turn peanut butter sandwiches into guns and want pet frogs. Our boys love working side by side with Dad in the garage, taking long walks in the woods, and spending hours playing with their Legos."

Amy knows full well the importance of raising her children with the tools to uphold one another's dignity. She teaches her boys to respect women not for what they look like but for who they are as daughters of God. Amy and her husband teach their children about modesty from a young age. "We have taught the boys to look away from immodestly dressed women and we teach all of our children to be extremely picky about what they watch, read, and listen to. This, in my opinion, is especially important for boys, who are inundated with images of scantily clad women everywhere they go," Amy pointed out. "We have taught our boys that just because these images are out there doesn't mean they have to look."

The images are indeed "out there," and studies show that males are more visually oriented than females. Unfortunately for many young boys today who are not being raised in a watchful Christian environment, pornography has become a foul and wounding preoccupation. With a few clicks of a mouse in the privacy of their own room or even on a cell phone, young boys can happen upon websites featuring all manner of porn—rape, torture, sadomasochism, and bestiality. Lord, have mercy on us!

One mother was upset about her daughter accidentally seeing

pornographic material on the cell phones of some eighth-grade boys at lunchtime. She took her concerns to a doctor, asking about the ramifications of this on the health and well-being of such young boys as well as on their future relationships with girls.

Dr. Michael Rich assured this mother that the scenario she described is not at all rare. He added that pornography affects everyone and "is a multibillion-dollar economic engine of the Internet, easily accessible with any Web-capable device. Combine that with the rapidly increasing ownership of and facility with cell phones by school-aged children, and you have the situation you describe."[5]

As for youth viewing pornography and how it may affect their ideas and attitudes about sex, Dr. Rich wrote: "Research with older adolescents and young adult males has shown that exposure to pornography results in objectification of, desensitization to, and reduced empathy for women. It also shows that men who view sexually explicit films degrading to women are more dominant in their subsequent interactions with women."[6]

According to an article in the *Sunday Times*, "Boys exposed to porn are more likely to indulge in casual sex and less likely to form successful relationships when they grow older, according to research carried out in a dozen countries."[7]

The same article mentions Michael Flood, who conducted a study titled "Harms of Pornography Exposure Among Children and Young People." The study revealed "that young boys who see pornography are more inclined to believe there is nothing wrong with pinning down or sexually harassing a girl."

"Porn is a very poor sex educator," Flood said, "because it shows sex in unrealistic ways and fails to address intimacy, love, connection, or romance. Often it is quite callous and hostile in its depictions of women."[8]

Research suggests that 60 percent of boys under sixteen have been exposed to pornography either accidentally or deliberately. In less than a decade, the average age when a boy first sees porn has dropped from fifteen to eleven. The average length of time boys watch porn on the Internet is said to be ninety minutes a week. Psychologist Petra Boynton adds the interesting observation that "children are not necessarily looking at porn for gratification. They are doing so because they are bored and not supervised."[9]

Why are young boys bored and unsupervised? It's not too hard to figure out. Too many parents are not present to their impressionable, vulnerable, curious kids and are much too permissive regarding the technology they allow them to use. Parents need to assign their kids some chores to do around the house, have higher expectations for their studies, and help them to become well-rounded in sports and the arts, all wholesome things. In other words, teach them Christian values and keep them busy and supervised! As our children's first and foremost educators, we will have to answer to God for all the idle unsupervised time we have selfishly doled out to our children, period.

If we look around we see all kinds of male fashion statements, from edgy hairstyles to piercings, tattoos, and zany clothing. As parents, we must choose our battles and discern what is dangerous to our children and what might be only their attempt to express their unique identity. While I believe we need to teach our children to respect their bodies as temples of the Holy Spirit, we need not have a conniption if our adult child comes home with a piercing.

One mom told me that she was in shock when her twenty-year-old son showed up with an eyebrow ring. She simply told him that she was very disappointed that he would choose to make holes in his face. She didn't say anything more about it. After a week, the ring became very uncomfortable and the piercing started to get infected—and that was the end of it. Let's use every opportunity to grow.

Despite the troubles in our culture and our need to be on the alert, raising boys is awesome. Each son enriches our lives in ways we could never have dreamed of. Thank God for the blessing of sons!

REFLECTION

Do you raise your sons and daughters with respect for their gifts and differences? What are some ways you accomplish this?

Do you respect your children's childhoods by not allowing them to be so influenced by the culture that they are robbed of essential developmental stages of growth? List some of the boundaries you've put in place.

Do you protect your children's innocence by being present to them and engaged in their lives as well as guarding them against the dangers lurking in today's ungodly culture? How have your children responded to this?

A PRAYER FOR THE JOURNEY

Dear Lord, please grant me the graces and wisdom to raise my sons and daughters in the way that is pleasing to you. Mother Mary, please guide me in my mothering and protect my family from the dangers of the world. Amen.

Dealing With Demands for Perfection

For all that is in the world—the desire of the flesh, the desire of the eyes, the pride in riches—comes not from the Father but from the world. And the world and its desire are passing away, but those who do the will of God live forever.

—1 John 2:16–18

THE SIMPLE FACT THAT WE are women subjects us to a myriad of expectations—from society, from our families, and from our peers. Unless we are hermits, these demands are all around us. The advertising world, for example, entices us to try this cream for a wrinkle-free complexion, this makeup for just the right glow, this diet product or exercise plan to be a size zero (is there really such a thing?).

Our goal as Christian women is to love and serve God, so let's take a look at some of the expectations we face on a daily basis, and let's explore what we can do about them.

Beginning with Girls

I want to look first at the societal pressures on young women, because I believe that this is where the demands for perfection start. As mothers, grandmothers, aunts, teachers, and friends, we can strive to make a positive difference in the lives of budding young women, confronting any unrealistic expectations we internalized in our own youth and turning our attention toward God's will for our lives. Young girls these days are subject to incredible demands from our culture. As parents, grandparents, aunts, and friends, we should recognize and try to address the difficulties our girls face. We should help to guide them safely into womanhood.

One of my friends had to send her teenaged daughter to a rehabilitation center to be treated for anorexia and drug abuse. Apparently no one saw this coming, which, sadly, is not rare. A sweet young girl from a churchgoing family, she simply couldn't deal with the demands of her peers, who portrayed a more appealing and exciting lifestyle. These girls taught her how to cleverly hide telltale signs from her parents. She barely escaped death, she later confessed. It was more than a year before she was able to return to her high school.

Everyday life for a teenager is tough enough as she has to struggle with hormonal mood swings—one minute exhilarated and the next minute immersed in a major trauma (acne, worry about boys, feeling that her parents just don't understand, academic pressures).

But today our culture tops it all off with crazy expectations that can be overwhelming. Sometimes life must seem like a pressure cooker to our impressionable young girls, who should be experiencing a positive and happy adolescence instead.

Statistics show that girls are three times more likely than boys to have a negative body image.[1] Adolescent girls are vulnerable, and they take criticisms personally and deeply. Feeling intimidated by the "in crowd," they may honestly think that they are fat or ugly. They might have to deal with bullies and kids who talk about them behind their backs.

It's impossible for us to miss the idealized female body image plastered all over mass media—Hollywood, the runway, television, and glossy magazines. Young girls and teens are brainwashed into believing that being a particular clothing size will bring them happiness and solve all of their problems. Most adolescents are unaware that what is projected to them as desirable is impossible to achieve anyway. The airbrushing used in the industry distorts a young girl's perception of what standard of physical beauty is realistically attainable.

There are other pressures on teens and tweens of both sexes. Consider all the pop stars, professional athletes, and actors and actresses who glamorize drug abuse and underage drinking. It's pretty scary to think that these celebrities masquerade as role models for children today.

What Can Parents Do?

First of all, the focus needs to be on a girl's real beauty—her talents, her mind, her heart, and her spirit as well as her natural grace and physique. Parents can start early to build self-esteem in their girls, to enable them to resist the battering of pressures as they grow. We can continue to show our affection even as they pull away during the adolescent years. We can respect their occasional need for solitude while welcoming and encouraging their participation in family activities and dinners.

A girl who feels loved by her parents and feels good about herself will still feel the pressures from our culture, but she will be better equipped to deal with them. Love is powerful! However, one study revealed that a mere 32 percent of girls felt loved by their parents.[2] This is alarming.

The best role models for kids are their parents. Our example speaks volumes. Our children look up to us and learn our behaviors. Something as small as prayers at the dinner table are not only wonderful, but essential—they set a valuable family tradition and fosters family values, as do get-togethers with relatives.

There's nothing like supportive girlfriends to help ease the trials and tribulations of being a teenager. Parents can steer their daughters away from cliques and toward wholesome friends. We can keep a close watch on our girls' activities and peer groups by encouraging get-togethers at our own homes, where we can have some control. It's important to know who our daughters are hanging out with. We can usually sense when something is not right. As parents, we have to trust our gut and then act.

I've watched my three daughters grow up, and I have always been cognizant of their choices of friends. I have enjoyed watching their interactions and hearing their lighthearted giggles during discussions of school and other activities. Taking an active role and interest in their lives has allowed me to discover what's going on and to be connected lovingly, even when they are away at college. I've done this with my two sons as well.

That we teach our girls not to worry about what others are saying and that we encourage them to be confident in their own skin is key. If we can reinforce this while they are very young, we will provide a solid and strong footing for them.

Clear and consistent boundaries provide parameters, establish a safety net, and help our children to make wise choices. Our kids actually want these guidelines, despite their attempts to rebel against them at times. Kids can even use their parents' rules as excuses to not get involved in potentially dangerous situations with their peers. It's a safe way out of trouble, and one that parents can suggest their children use.

Our continual open communication and encouragement will reassure our daughters, nieces, and granddaughters that they can come to us with their troubles and their joys. We may discover opportunities for meaningful conversation while out on a walk, driving in the car, or participating in an activity with them. They may be more likely to open up in such situations rather than in face-to-face encounters, which can be awkward. Prayer and inspiration from the Holy Spirit will unveil opportunities for this.

To guide them through these years safely, we absolutely have to show young girls our love in affectionate, understanding, and tangible ways and really be there for them—always! It's up to us to be examples of how to live in this world without being subject to its demands (see John 17:11–19). We must learn the way to the Father ourselves and then show them the way!

The "Perfect" Woman

Christian women are not exempt from the stresses of various demands for perfection. Sorting through all the mixed messages can be a daunting task. In addition, women can be a bit competitive, oftentimes sizing themselves up against other women. Oh, what a tangled web!

Let's get down to the nitty-gritty. What are some of the pressures we as women deal with?

It seems to me that we all face demands for perfection to a certain degree in the home, the workplace, the community, and beyond. A laundry list of questions comes to mind when considering what signifies *perfection*.

Is it the house you own or its aesthetics?

Is it the number of children you have, how well they behave, or their grades?

Is it the classes you take at the gym, your youthful, wrinkle-free, toned body, or your perfect manicure?

Does being *perfect* have anything to do with your spouse, his salary, his attitude toward you, or his involvement with the family?

Could it have something to do with where you went to school, the prestigious committees you are on, the number of zeros in your salary, or the books you are reading?

Could it even be about your closeness to the Lord or how much you pray?

Sounds crazy maybe; however, all of these are real pressures for today's women, whether they are conscious of them or not. We face the enormous task of deciphering the tangle of confusing messages that are aimed at us and make us wonder how we can be more perfect women.

Ironically, women who struggle for perfection can find themselves feeling less and less adequate. They buy into the world's notions about their worth and struggle to keep up with what society expects of them rather than heed what their hearts tell them. They worry about everything from their appearance to their place in society, often leaving their children to the care of others in order to prove their worth to the world. They join endless committees or spend small fortunes on their appearance and the decor of their homes, only to end up in the therapist's office, looking for peace of mind and wondering why they aren't happy and why they aren't perfect.

To Live a Vibrant Life

Will we listen to the demands of our culture, or will we listen to our hearts and holy Mother Church?

It's tough to sift through all that comes at us. But we must discern what really matters and what things are merely distractions that can knock us off the narrow path that leads to heaven. Facing the facts, we are not going to find encouragement for genuine femininity from the outrageous television shows and glossy magazines that our world offers.

Yes, the evil one is involved in all of it. He wants to demean and exploit women. I don't think we need a reminder about what happened when Eve listened to him and fell into his trap.

It is helpful to consider who will influence our decisions. Who are our role models?

To me, my mother seemed to be the perfect woman. She and my father raised eight children attentively. Her hands were too busy for a manicure—always washing dishes, taking care of the house, changing diapers, cooking for her brood, or cleaning up after us. Because she clothed her children first, she rarely wore fashionable clothes.

By today's standards my mother would be considered less than perfect, yet she was perfect in my eyes. She always knew what was troubling us, and she gave us her warm shoulder with an abundance of support and love. She helped us with our studies and guided us in prayer.

We can turn to our Blessed Mother for help in sorting through the demands for perfection in our lives and discerning what God wants of us. Mother Mary is certainly a superb model of a *perfect* woman whom we can strive to follow. We'll discuss her more in the next chapter.

Focusing on the clear, understandable, and encouraging words from our Church will help direct our thoughts toward heaven and its rewards. Again, I encourage Catholic women to read *Mulieris Dignitatem,* the amazing apostolic letter of Bl. John Paul II on the dignity and vocation of women, and to pray and ponder its affirming words. "A woman's dignity," John Paul wrote, "is closely connected with the love which she receives by the very reason of her femininity; it is likewise connected *with the love which she gives in return.... Woman can only find herself by giving love to others.*"[3]

I have seen many women turn misty-eyed on hearing the pope's words. We are fortunate to be blessed with our innate femininity, born in hearts that are meant to be generous—hearts that can help to heal wounds, bridge gaps, and soothe the "savage beast" by God's grace and our submission to his holy will. Let us pray that all women will discover their true, God-given femininity. This is the prayer of the pope and of the Church.

John Paul in *Mulieris Dignitatem continues:*

> The Church gives thanks *for all the manifestations of the feminine "genius"* which have appeared in the course of history, in the midst of all peoples and nations; she gives thanks for all the charisms which the Holy Spirit distributes to women in the history of the People of God, for all the victories which she owes to their faith, hope and charity: she gives thanks for all *the fruits of feminine holiness.*
>
> … Meditating on the biblical mystery of the "woman," the Church prays that in this mystery all women may discover themselves and their "supreme vocation." [4]

So let's do that. Let's pray that, through God's grace, we can discover our "supreme vocation." Let's ask our Lord to help us unearth the beauty and richness of our femininity and our "feminine genius," so that we can receive his love and courageously pass it on to our families and communities. And let's spread this message to those around us as well as to future generations.

A Time to Ponder and Pray

Take a few moments to ponder the beauty of the feminine genius. Pray to the Holy Spirit for inspiration, and ask our Lord to enlighten your mind with a greater awareness of your feminine gifts. Ask him to grant you an increase in the virtues of faith, hope, and love.

At the beginning of this chapter, we read words from 1 John regarding worldly desires and promises, which will pass away, as opposed to our Lord's promises, which are eternal. With that in mind, prayerfully consider the questions below.

R E F L E C T I O N

What can you do about the demands for perfection in your life? What *will* you do?

What can you do about the unrealistic demands aimed at young girls whom you may influence? What *will* you do?

How can you tap into your *fruits of feminine holiness* that Bl. John Paul II spoke of?

A   P R A Y E R   F O R   T H E   J O U R N E Y

Dear Lord Jesus, help me to keep my eyes on you. Save me from falling into the trap of the evil one, worrying about satisfying everyone else's demands and losing sight of you and what is really important. Please enlighten my mind and increase the virtues of faith, hope, and love in my heart. Open my heart to a new and greater awareness of my God-given feminine gifts.

Please inspire me to be a holy and wholesome example to young girls and other women, so that I may prayerfully draw them all closer to you, by your grace. Mother Mary, please be at my side. Amen.

CHAPTER SEVEN

The Blessed Mother as Our Model for Holiness

May it be done to me according to your word.

—Luke 1:38, *NAB*

BL. TERESA OF CALCUTTA WROTE: "The wonderful tenderness of a woman's heart: to be aware of the suffering of others and to try to spare them that suffering, as Mary did. Do you and I have that same tenderness in our hearts? Do we have Mary's eyes for discovering the needs of others?"[1]

Recalling various scenarios in Mary's life, we reflect on her gentleness, humility, holiness, perseverance, selflessness, and unwavering faith. We wonder, Can a woman like me aspire to emulate such an amazing woman—the Virgin Mother of God, the first disciple, the matriarch of the Holy Family, and the mother of the Church?

I ask myself this question because I know I will never accomplish what our Blessed Mother has or even come close to her holiness. Yet all women are called to holiness—whether in the sublime role of raising children, as a wife, as a single woman, or as a consecrated woman or a religious. Mary demonstrates attributes and virtues that all women can emulate, whatever their vocation.

Mary's deep faith was the foundation of her great holiness. Even though Mary was the Mother of God, we should remember that she was also human like us and prayed to be unwavering in her faith, just as we also are called to do. Mary's faith is the same gift available to us. We can ask God for an increase in faith and ask Mary to be a mother to us and guide us closer to her son, Jesus.

A Faithful Heart

Wanting to imitate Mary's virtues, we may try to figure out what made her tick. Perhaps images from our Catholic tradition and Scripture come to mind. We may be reminded of Mary as a faithful Jewish girl praying with her people in Palestine for the coming of the Messiah, the fulfillment of God's promises. Mary was very familiar with Isaiah's words that a virgin would conceive and bear a child called Immanuel—"God with us"—but never imagined that *she* would be that woman.

At times, we might find ourselves in situations requiring faith in God, but our humanness causes us to feel inadequate or to fear that we are not faithful enough. When, ten weeks pregnant with my fifth child, I hemorrhaged profusely, I was required to have faith that God's holy will would be fulfilled, whatever it would be.

My doctor told me that I was miscarrying. He conducted an

ultrasound to check on the baby. When the ultrasound revealed a tiny baby with a beating heart, I was ordered to stay on complete bed rest and just wait. The doctor added that he wished the miscarriage would hurry up, saving me from further anguish.

I shuddered at his words and chose to hope and pray instead. I rested and waited and never stopped praying. My four children bustled around me as I did my best to stay still and have faith in whatever it was that God had planned for us. I knew Bl. Teresa of Calcutta personally at the time, and she instructed me to wear the Miraculous Medal she had given me and to call on the Blessed Mother. She reminded me to trust in our Lord, stay close to Mary, and pray, "Mary, Mother of Jesus, be a mother to me now."

My prayers were heard, and after a long nine months Mary-Catherine was born! In retrospect, I can understand why our Lord may have given me more than one reason to pause during that pregnancy: While I was kept still, I was inspired to write about motherhood. These reflections have since been published in several books. As a busy mother with four children and another on the way, I might never have had a spare moment to sit down to write, never mind even think about doing it! Our Lord knew what he was doing.

Humble Generosity and Courage

We know that when the angel Gabriel visited Mary with the announcement that she would become Jesus' mother (see Luke 1:26–39), the humble teenager found it difficult to believe that it was she, a simple girl, who had been chosen by God. Taking the blessing to heart, Mary responded with her courageous "Yes" to God.

Shortly afterward, her generous heart sent her on a journey into the hill country, pregnant and "in haste," to help her cousin Elizabeth, who was much older and also expecting a child (see Luke 1:39). Mary surely prayed and reflected throughout her journey while the blessedness of Jesus dwelled within her. After Elizabeth's baby leaped in her womb on Mary's arrival, the two women embraced. Elizabeth praised Mary for her great faith, and Mary humbly responded with the words of the Magnificat, glorifying God's holiness, justice, and mercy and foretelling that all generations would call her blessed because of the great things the Lord had done for her (see Luke 1:46–55).

When we question our own ability to courageously answer God with our own "Yes" when he bids us to follow him, we must remember that, as women, we are also blessed with generous and courageous hearts like Mary's. Graces are available to us to be bold and brave and to respond with love in all situations within our vocations. Throughout our daily lives, we are presented with many opportunities to put our own needs aside and go "in haste" to help—our children, our spouses, our parents, our neighbors, our coworkers, or whomever God has put into our lives. How will we respond?

The Simplicity of Love

Mary was led on a donkey by her beloved husband, Joseph, in search of a place to give birth and met only rejection by the innkeepers. Soon afterward, the crying infant Jesus was comforted at his mother's breast in a stable. Our Savior was born into poverty, resting in a wooden manger of hay—hardly what one would expect for a king's birth! Angels sent simple shepherds to Mary and Joseph to see their holy baby. Mary "kept all these things, pondering them in her heart" (Luke 2:19).

When we face rejection in one form or another, we can pray for the graces we need to continue on, just as Mary did in Bethlehem and then later, when she felt the sting of her son's rejection by the very people he helped. We can imagine Mary throughout the hidden years, teaching Jesus on her knee in the warmth of their humble home. As Jesus grew, Mary surely encouraged her son to help St. Joseph in his carpentry. Mary's faith deepened in the cenacle of prayer that she fostered in the heart of her home.

Mothers, too, live through hidden years, raising their families and trying to remain simple as their faith grows. Especially when children are young, mothers may find themselves housebound owing to the care of the family, children's illnesses, or infants too small to go out. A mother can make her home a domestic church by praying with her children, teaching them about the faith, and thanking God for the blessedness of her family and the opportunity to care for it.

"Do Whatever He Tells You"

At the start of Jesus' public ministry, feeling sympathy for a bride and groom who would run out of wine for their guests, Mary told Jesus, "They have no wine." While Jesus appeared reluctant to perform his first miracle, saying that his hour had not yet come, Mary confidently told the wine stewards to "do whatever he tells you" (John 2:2–11). Mary's initiative, intercession, and obedience ultimately urged on her Son. And so the power of a mother's love brought about Jesus' first public miracle.

Women, as mothers, have within reach the tremendous power of prayer. A mother has the ability to influence her children for better or for worse. A faithful mother's prayers will always be heard by God. In their intercessory role, faithful mothers are forever praying for the welfare of their children, both for those living at home and for those who are grown and may have strayed away from the Church. A mother's prayers can be just as efficacious as those of our Blessed Mother, and they too have the power to work miracles in human hearts.

The Heart of the Home

Women can learn from Mary as one who listened to God and allowed the Holy Spirit to inspire and guide her. She gave herself completely to the will of the Father. We learn from Mary that a mother's prayer is powerful. When we are asked to endure suffering or pain within our vocation, we can turn our thoughts to Mother Mary, who was no stranger to suffering, and ask for her assistance and intercession.

When it is difficult to trust in God, we can meditate on Mary's faithful trust in our Lord, drawing strength from her as we pray for guidance from the Holy Spirit. When those of us who are mothers experience deep joy within our role, we can feel an affinity with someone who has also experienced this deep joy in mothering Jesus.

Mary's marvelous "Yes" to God changed the entire world for all eternity. May all faithful women also courageously answer our Lord with the words, "Let it be done to me according to your word," as they strive to live holy lives and raise their families in a cenacle of prayer fostered in their domestic churches, pondering it all deep within their own hearts and setting an example for women everywhere.

Marian Prayers and Devotions

The *Catechism* explains that "in prayer the Holy Spirit unites us to the person of the only Son, in his glorified humanity, through which and in which our filial prayer unites us in the Church with the Mother of Jesus (see Acts 1:14)."[2]

Praying a family rosary may seem like a daunting task, especially when there are rambunctious little ones, a shortage of time, and perhaps even a lack of interest. However, this beautiful, age-old prayer is worth every effort. Many popes and saints have remarked about its efficacy. It's wise to establish this very fruitful prayer habit of praying the rosary when the children are young so that it will become an integral part of their lives, something they are accustomed to.

The rosary can be broken up into decades, which makes it much more doable with your sometimes distracted crew. In time, an additional decade can be added to your repertoire until you've got a full rosary together under your belts.

I love what Bl. John Paul II in *Rosarium Virginis Mariae*, when he was then a beloved pope, said about the rosary. "With the rosary, the Christian people *sit at the school of Mary* and are led to contemplate the beauty on the face of Christ and to experience the depths of his love. Through the rosary the faithful receive abundant grace, as though from the very hands of the Mother of the Redeemer."[3]

Near the end of this apostolic letter, Bl. John Paul II presents us with a challenge. He said, "I look to all of you, brothers and sisters of every state of life, to you, Christian families, to you, the sick and elderly, and to you, young people: *confidently take up the rosary once again*. Rediscover the rosary in the light of Scripture, in harmony with the Liturgy, and in the context of your daily lives."[4]

His appeal to us along with the splendid promise of abundant graces straight from our dear Blessed Mother should be more than enough to persuade us to pick up the beads and get our family to do the same—hopefully together.

The *Catechism* teaches us that "Mary is the perfect *Orans* (prayer), a figure of the Church. When we pray to her, we are adhering with her to the plan of the Father, who sends his Son to save all men. Like the beloved disciple, we welcome Jesus' mother into our homes, for she has become the mother of all the living. We can pray with and to her. The prayer of the Church is sustained by the prayer of Mary and united with it in hope."[5]

Below are some popular and powerful prayers to Mary.

The Canticle of Mary (or Magnificat)

My soul proclaims the greatness of the Lord,
    my spirit rejoices in God my Savior,
for he has looked with favor on his lowly servant.
From this day all generations will call me blessed:
the Almighty has done great things for me,
    and holy is his Name.
He has mercy on those who fear him
    in every generation.

He has shown the strength of his arm,
  he has scattered the proud in their conceit.
He has cast down the mighty from their thrones,
  and has lifted up the lowly.
He has filled the hungry with good things,
  and the rich he has sent away empty.
He has come to the help of his servant Israel,
  for he remembered his promise of mercy,
the promise he made to our fathers,
  to Abraham and his children for ever.

The text of the Canticle of Mary, or the Magnificat, is taken from Luke 1:46–55 and is sung each evening to celebrate evening prayer.

The Memorare

Remember, O most gracious Virgin Mary,
  that never was it known that anyone who fled to your
    protection,
  implored your help, or sought your intercession, was left
    unaided.
Inspired by this confidence, I fly unto you, O Virgin of virgins,
  my Mother.
To you I come, before you I stand, sinful and sorrowful.
O Mother of the Word incarnate, despise not my petitions,
    but, in your mercy, hear and answer me. Amen.

The Memorare (meaning *Remember*) is a personal petition of prayer to our Blessed Mother asking for her powerful intercession. It is a favorite prayer of many. Bl. Teresa of Calcutta prayed this prayer often. In fact, she prayed it nine times in a row in the form of a novena whenever she placed an urgent request before the Blessed Mother.

Hail Mary

Hail Mary, full of grace, the Lord is with thee!
Blessed art thou among women, and blessed is the fruit of thy
  womb, Jesus.
Holy Mary, Mother of God, pray for us sinners,
  now and at the hour of our death. Amen.

For centuries, the Hail Mary has been prayed all throughout the rosary. It is also the heart of the Angelus prayer. It originates from the first chapter of the Gospel of Luke: the "angelic salutation" of the angel Gabriel to the Virgin Mary—"Hail, full of grace, the Lord is with you" (Luke 1:28)—the announcement that she was to become the mother of the Son of God. And from Elizabeth as she greeted her cousin, exclaiming, "Blessed are you among women, and blessed is the fruit of thy womb!" before going on to ask, "And why is this granted me, that the mother of my Lord should come to me?" (Luke 1:42, 43). Mary then cries out her jubilant hymn of praise, the Magnificat, or the Canticle of Mary (see above).

The Angelus

The Angel of the Lord declared to Mary:
And she conceived of the Holy Spirit.
Hail Mary, full of grace, the Lord is with thee; blessed art thou
  among women and blessed is the fruit of thy womb, Jesus. Holy

Mary, Mother of God, pray for us sinners, now and at the hour of our death. Amen.

Behold the handmaid of the Lord: Be it done unto me according to thy word.

Hail Mary ...

And the Word was made flesh, and dwelt among us.

Hail Mary ...

Pray for us, O Holy Mother of God, that we may be made worthy of the promises of Christ.

Let us pray:

Pour forth, we beseech thee, O Lord, thy grace into our hearts; that we, to whom the incarnation of Christ thy Son was made known by the message of an angel, may by his passion and cross be brought to the glory of his resurrection, through the same Christ our Lord. Amen.

Church bells are traditionally rung in three bursts of three chimes (with a slight pause between rings). It is followed by nine consecutive strokes of bells at three different parts of the day: 6 AM, noon, and 6 PM. This tradition springs from the monastic practice of praying matins, prime, and compline (the *tres orations*). The bells were a reminder to the people in the village that prayers were being said by the monastics, allowing the faithful to pause briefly in their work to pray three Hail Marys in honor of the Incarnation in union with the monks. Verses were added to the three Hail Marys sometime around the year 1612.

During the Easter season (Paschaltide), the Angelus is replaced with the Regina Coeli (below) because it is more joyous. Pope Benedict XIV directed this change in 1742.

The famous masterpiece *The Angelus* by Jean-Francois Millet depicts two young peasants who stop their work in a potato field to bow their heads and pray the Angelus. The Angelus bells are said to be ringing from the steeple of the church building on the horizon. Many say that the painting radiates a deep feeling of prayer.

Regina Coeli

Queen of Heaven, rejoice, alleluia. / For he whom you did merit to bear, alleluia. / Has risen, as he said, alleluia. / Pray for us to God, alleluia.

Rejoice and be glad, O Virgin Mary, alleluia. / For the Lord has truly risen, alleluia.

Let us pray. O God, who gave joy to the world through the resurrection of thy Son, our Lord Jesus Christ, grant, we beseech thee, that through the intercession of the Virgin Mary, his Mother, we may obtain the joys of everlasting life. Through the same Christ our Lord. Amen.

Legend claims that St. Gregory the Great (d. 604) heard the first three lines of the Regina Coeli chanted by angels on an Easter morning as he was walking in a religious procession. He is said to have added the fourth line: "Ora pro nobis Deum. Alleluia."[6]

There are countless prayers to Mary our Mother. Many popes and saints have composed prayers to her. Added to that are numerous litanies to Mary, novena prayers, prayers of consecration, prayers of the saints and spiritual writers, and various chaplet prayers. There's no doubt about it, the Blessed Mother is beloved to an incalculable number of souls. Bl. John Paul the Great himself wrote more than forty prayers to the Blessed Mother. He lived by the words *totus tuus,* which means "totally yours." These words were included on his coat of arms, as this beloved pope had an intense love for the Mother of Christ. We know that both Bl. John Paul the Great and Bl. Teresa of Calcutta used the formula of St. Louis de Montfort (author of *True Devotion to Mary)* to consecrate themselves to Jesus through Mary.

REFLECTION

Do you seek intercession from the Blessed Mother for help, grace, and comfort? Do you ask her to bring you closer to her son, Jesus?

Do you teach your children to pray to Mary? What are some of the ways you've found to help your children foster a devotion to her?

How can you emulate some of the Blessed Mother's virtues?

A PRAYER FOR THE JOURNEY

Dear Lord, Jesus, thank you for the gift of your holy Mother. Dear Mother Mary, please guide me always in my mothering and teach me to emulate your virtues. Amen.

CHAPTER EIGHT

Dealing With the Really Difficult Stuff

When you encounter difficulties and contradictions, do not try to break them, but bend them with gentleness and time.

—St. Francis de Sales, *Introduction to the Devout Life*

BEING A MOTHER IS UNQUESTIONABLY a very holy and joyful vocation. After all, what other vocation cooperates with God to bring human life into the world? What other vocation is blessed with the gift of growing along with our children as we raise them? Even so, some mothers experience much more joy than others. Some mothers have to endure a good deal of hardship in their lives, for whatever reason. Only our good Lord knows for sure. Yet, with God's grace, those challenged mothers can come through the "splinters from the Cross" with renewed faith, hope, and love. One can hope that they will then be able to offer comfort and strength to others who are struggling.

We'll look at a variety of trying situations throughout this chapter. Perhaps you'll find yourself here or you may know someone who is in the same boat as someone here. With God's grace, we can try in some way to lend our hands and hearts to any mothers who must undergo such suffering so that they may begin to feel more hopeful about their plight and perhaps even begin to see the light at the end of the tunnel.

Losing One's Child

"My baby! My baby!" Her cries sliced through the painful silence in the church like a freshly sharpened dagger. The tears turned to mournful sobbing when all who were present heard the cries of this distraught mother whose daughter's coffin was being wheeled down the aisle and out of the church toward the cemetery. Those words uttered from a mother's agonizing heart echo in mine even now. I couldn't possibly imagine her pain, but hearing her desperate call to her dead daughter was unsettling and caused my heart to feel like it was breaking for the poor woman. I'll never forget that moment as long as I live.

I can't think of anything worse for a mother than losing her child, whether it's through a miscarriage or after the child is born. I myself have suffered three miscarriages, and I have to believe that my innocent babies went straight into the arms of Jesus and Mary.

My dear friend Angela lost her twenty-year-old son, Christopher, in a car accident. Another son, Joseph, was also in the car and sustained serious injuries. My own maternal heart couldn't possibly fathom the pain that Angela, her other children, and her husband, Andy, were enduring. I felt utterly crushed on hearing the news and wanted to run immediately to their sides to embrace them.

How did this family cope? It wasn't merely their Catholic faith *getting* them through the misfortune—their faith seemed to *carry* them through! Angela stood strong at the funeral Mass as she gave a eulogy for her own son. I don't know of many mothers who could do that. Christopher's sisters spoke about their beloved brother as well. To see the miraculous grace lived through this heartbroken family was indeed edifying. Tears came to my eyes as I observed the family downstairs in the parish hall after the funeral. Andrew, the oldest brother, who was about to go off to the seminary, was pushing his injured brother Joseph in a wheelchair around the hall, while family members and friends, one by one, spontaneously joined in a line behind them as the words from the song "When the Saints Go Marching In" were belted out—with smiling faces and joyous laughter!

Unplanned Pregnancies and the Temptation to Abort

It may seem odd that I am discussing abortion in a book clearly meant to be about embracing Catholic motherhood. But I must raise this important issue here to open our eyes to the reality that exists in many women's lives. Some mothers are raising children whom they may not have necessarily planned on raising, such as in the case of rape or premarital sex. Some mothers have even contemplated aborting their unborn child. With all the cultural pressure and economic problems these days, a woman's thoughts may turn to suicide, sometimes feeling that she doesn't have much choice and has nowhere to turn.

Faith, a young international college student, told me she wanted to "end it all" when she learned that she had conceived after being raped.[1] She had no one she could turn to in a foreign country. But Faith knew in her heart that, as much as she felt frightened about the future and wasn't sure what to do, she couldn't destroy a human life. As soon as she found out she was pregnant, she went to a chapel to pray. It was there that she decided she would give her baby up for adoption. She was also very fortunate that her college was located near a pro-life pregnancy clinic, where she eventually received much support, both physically and emotionally. When baby Isaac was placed in his mother's arms, Faith again changed her mind, this time to keep him and raise him herself. "I knew I didn't want to let him go," she said. Faith and her son are doing well.

Faith will no doubt experience difficulties as a single mother as she raises her son. She told me that it's tough to find someone to watch him while she's in her college classes, which she attends part-time. She fears what sort of wrath she may face from her not-so-understanding family when she returns to her country. I give Faith and other single mothers a lot of credit for doing their best to mother and "father" their children. I don't know many single mothers who *choose* to parent alone. Let's not judge them; let's pray for them instead!

A single mother named Georgia shared her incredible story with me. She began, "I survived the overwhelming temptation to abort this precious little being. Or, shall I say, this baby survived my temptation."

Georgia became pregnant through premarital sex. "I felt I was a walking contradiction the first week I discovered I was pregnant," she said. "After all, I had become strongly pro-life in my early thirties, volunteering at my local pro-life office and marching in D.C. for the unborn. I used to say, 'How could women even contemplate killing their child?' Now I understand to a degree that I never thought I would what really goes on inside the mind of a woman who is thinking of doing the unthinkable."

Georgia later decided she would give her baby up for adoption rather than abort her. She was living in a dangerous situation and had to flee to another state to protect herself and her unborn baby from abuse just seven days before her due date. She was frightened and crying because she had to go to an unfamiliar hospital with new doctors. While enduring the uncertainty, she was hit with another blow. Just hours before she went into labor, the adoption plans fell through.

"I thought I'd been through worse in my life, having been neglected, abused, and abandoned as a child, in and out of foster homes, homeless, addicted to drugs and alcohol as a teenager, and struggling to survive." Now Georgia faced this unplanned pregnancy, her biggest challenge by far.

Georgia says, "It took the entire decade of my twenties to overcome my childhood nightmares and yet nothing, absolutely nothing, compares to the horror of contemplating abortion."

During her pregnancy, providentially she felt stirred by an image of Our Lady of Guadalupe. "It snapped me out of that terribly dark place," she said. "I just love her." She explained: "After the replica came to my church, I began praying to God for two things: to know his will and then to have the strength to fulfill it. I lived totally and one hundred percent in the present moment. And, miraculously, during the most difficult time of my life, I felt and continue to feel an unbelievable sense of peace. Now, I wholeheartedly believe that God can bless any mess."

Georgia added, "If there is one thing I learned from the temptation to abort my baby, it is this: Women do not feel they have 'freedom of choice' when they think of killing the gift from God growing inside of them. They think of doing it precisely because they feel they have *no* choice!"

Georgia praises God every day for the strength and grace he gave her to say "Yes!" to giving her little Gianna Maria life. "Every time I nurse her, I thank him for giving me the courage to 'be not afraid,' as Pope John Paul II used to say."

Both Faith and Georgia are brave women, turning to prayer and, with God's grace, overcoming extremely challenging circumstances to welcome new life. May God bless them! They are just two of the countless women out there who have experienced fear, trauma, and uncertainty in their plights. Many women in such circumstances do not have the foundation of prayer to provide them with strength or to bring them out of a dark place. We must pray for them and, if possible, help them.

Raising a Special-Needs Child

Raising a special-needs child comes with challenges, sacrifices, and joys. The news a parent receives about the state of their child either before birth or afterward can be devastating and frightening.

Eileen, mother to twelve-year-old daughter, Sadie, declined prenatal testing and learned that her little girl had Down syndrome when she was placed in her arms shortly after birth.

Eileen says that, although she had never seen a baby with Down syndrome, "As soon as I looked at her beautiful face, I just knew. It seemed that she told me with her eyes. For an instant, I felt that my whole life was meant for this experience." She adds, "If I had heard the doctor's words first, I might have been more shocked."

"If I were to name one challenge, I would say that it is having patience. I am a fast-paced person, and having Sadie has forced me to slow down, whether it is out and about shopping or waiting for her to get ready to go out."

Sadie's birth was actually the catalyst that eventually led Eileen back to the Catholic faith. "I knew she was a unique gift from God, one that not everyone is privileged to experience," Eileen shares. Prayer, the sacraments, the rosary, and Catholic writings give her strength in raising her family. "Of course, I often fall short, but these things are still there to help me along my way."

Eileen recognizes that "while other children grow up and live independent lives, Sadie's care and safety will always be our responsibility." Nonetheless, Eileen says, "Sadie is a joy, and I want to be there for her."

Leticia, mother of eight-year-old Christina, who also has Down syndrome, shared some disturbing facts. "When trisomy 21 [the medical term for the condition] is diagnosed prenatally there is a 92 percent abortion rate. Most mothers are quickly pressured into 'making the appointment' [for an abortion] as soon as the diagnosis is given, without time to think or discuss with their spouse. They are given negative, outdated information, told their child will never speak, read, or tie their shoes, and advised that the compassionate thing for their other children, spouse, and the disabled child is to end his or her life." Because of this, Leticia laments, "There are very few playmates for my daughter in her school who resemble her. This is a great loss to society because it is based on a lie." Leticia finds comfort in her Catholic faith and offers her emotional and prayer support to parents facing the same diagnosis.

Allison and her husband adopted their daughter Faith, who is profoundly deaf, when she was four years old. Allison pointed out that our world "is not designed for the hearing-impaired." She added, "Although we are blessed to live at a time with amazing technological advances to aid Faith's communication, we know the road ahead for her will be long." As an early-childhood educator, she knows that the first three years of life are critical for learning, and because Faith was given no communication for those first four years, Allison is also dealing with delays from not receiving any literacy or language. Because friends and family often ask Allison to teach them sign language so they can communicate with Faith, Allison offers a weekly sign-language class at her home.

Eucharistic Adoration brings Allison tremendous peace in her mothering as she homeschools Faith, a son with ADD, and a middle child with a cognitive processing disorder. "My faith is my life, and without it I truly know I would never have even ventured into adopting a child, never mind one with special needs," Allison explains. She said she really feels the power of prayer and can tell "when we've been lifted in prayer. We can handle whatever their special needs bring, but only through our prayers and the prayers of others!" she adds.

Parenting Alone

I think it's rare for a mother to want to parent alone. However, I do know some single women who have chosen to adopt a child on their own. In most cases, however, parenting a child is best accomplished by a mother and a father.

We know that there are countless mothers in our world today who are single for a variety of reasons. Some have never been married, some are divorced, and others are widows. I was a single mother for many years, so I totally understand the many difficulties of raising children alone—as well as the stigma that often comes along with it.

Educating children spiritually is another area in which mothers may parent alone, or perhaps feel that they are parenting alone, which can happen in the case of a disinterested or not so prayerful husband. Many Catholic and Christian mothers lament that they are basically raising their children in the faith single-handedly, because their husbands either aren't much help or refuse to have any part of it. Perhaps they are unbelievers or lack a real commitment to the faith. The burden then falls squarely on the shoulders of the faithful mother. It can be exhausting and disheartening.

Sue, a Catholic mother of six, expressed it this way: "Not having your 'better half' entirely on your side in the faith formation of the children can be a huge challenge. I know it affects the children a lot, and it's sort of like going upstream." She went on to say, "Probably one of the hardest things about being in a mixed-marriage situation is that you desire to have that spiritual bond with your spouse. You want to share the one most important thing in your life and yet you can't." Because of this huge separation of beliefs, Sue feels she needs to be "a better outward example in the faith in order to combat anything that is contrary to the faith" from her husband.

Sue's husband doesn't attend Mass. The family feels the loss, and the younger kids often question why their dad won't go. "It is very confusing to them," she explained. "As they get older, they start to realize that Church is more of a choice, and so they start to question their own faith and reasons to attend Mass." Sue feels fortunate that her husband has agreed to use natural family planning, but she still sometimes struggles with him over it. "He often hears from his friends and relatives that he should get 'fixed,' and this puts a lot of pressure on him."

Challenges abound for Catholic mothers like Sue, who says she feels like a single parent and wonders "if people are judging me or assuming I'm a woman who had kids out of wedlock. I sometimes try to make my wedding ring quite visible so that people see that I am, indeed, married." Many times she leaves the youngest at home with her husband, since trying to handle them all of them herself at Mass is nearly impossible.

Prayer at home is a thorny issue as well for Sue. "At first my husband was very open to prayer at mealtimes. He wouldn't participate, but he didn't mind. Then it started to become awkward because the children would question why Daddy wasn't involved. So meal prayers were dropped," she confessed. Raising her kids Catholic "basically comes down to trying to do religious activities with the children when my husband is not in the room. It can be like hiding something from one's spouse, because it becomes an uncomfortable situation for one or both."

Many times Sue feels like she's "barely hanging on, barely clinging to that thread of instruction that my children need because as a mom I'm overworked in everything. I cook, clean, tend to the babies, and deal with my own pregnancy problems, which cause great exhaustion, physical pain, or discomfort. And as a mother—there is always a lack of sleep!"

She undoubtedly knows that all of the above affects her ability to pass on the faith. "When I am too tired, prayers can be forgotten," she said. "When I am trying to get the children ready for church in the morning, it can be one big stress-filled event that does not end until we are home from Mass and I can breathe a sigh of relief that my 'duty' was done."

Inspiration from the saints gives Sue strength, and she finds solace among her Catholic friends. She often ponders the verse "Lord, to whom shall we go? You have the words of eternal life" (John 6:68). She believes that "despite all of the hardships, shortcomings, and failings of my own life and situation, there really is no other way to go. I love the Church, and I hope that love will rub off on my children even if they have only 'half' an example in their home life. My faith is not diminished, but I do feel inadequate doing it all by myself." Despite the difficulties, Sue said, "I think God opened that gate because he knew that a faithful spouse may help bring the pagan spouse into the Church. This is my dream, and it's a prayer I say every night."

Teens and Sexual Promiscuity
In a culture where a prevailing sex-education agenda advocates sexual intimacy as being perfectly fine at whatever age a person feels is right for him or her, it is no wonder that there are so many cases of sexually transmitted diseases (STDs) today as well as babies born out of wedlock and babies killed in the act of abortion.

Today, despite supposed "safe sex," there are at least twenty-five varieties of STDs. The American Social Health Association reports that 750,000 Americans carry human papillomavirus and four million people have contracted chlamydia. The twenty-five-year-old-and-younger crowd is hardest hit to the tune of contracting two-thirds of all STDs. Part of the reason that girls under the age of twenty are affected by sexually transmitted diseases is that their cervix is not mature enough for sex. The thin transformation zone at that age makes them more susceptible to problems and diseases. As a woman's body matures, the cervix thickens and offers better protection.

"Dr. Anonymous," aka Miriam Grossman, M.D., a psychiatrist working at UCLA and the author of *Unprotected: A Campus Psychiatrist Reveals How Political Correctness in Her Profession Endangers Every Student*, writes of her concerns about the dire state of campus life. Specifically, she said in an interview at *National Review Online*, "Depending on the study, 40–80 percent of [college] students 'hook-up,' and by graduation, the average number of these nearly anonymous encounters is ten. Yet we wonder why so many young people suffer from depression, anxiety, eating disorders, and self-abuse." Hooking up, she explains, is defined as "sexual encounters in which there is no expectation of seeing one another again."

Dr. Grossman explained:

> A young woman is not warned that she is hard-wired to attach through sexual behavior, and that no condom will protect her from the heartache and confusion that may

result. Also missing from her education is that the younger she is, the more vulnerable her system is to infection with a sexually transmitted virus or bacteria. Some of these organisms are transmitted even with condom use, and may have painful consequences even with timely diagnosis and treatment. This is information every incoming freshman must know; it will optimize her chances of staying emotionally and physically healthy as she navigates her way through the anything-goes campus environment.

Our universities and health organizations have yet to declare war on the hook-up culture, and some campuses actually promote and glorify it. I suggest parents log on to Columbia University's goaskalice.com for a sense of how some schools normalize risky behaviors. This is especially hazardous for a young woman, who may feel pressure to fit in. The university and health organizations advise her to limit her partners, use condoms, and get tested frequently for STDs. In doing so, they say, she'll be "safe," or at least "safer."[2]

An issue we may not hear much about is how the powerful hormone oxytocin can wreak havoc with and cause confusion in youth and their feelings about intimacy. I've written about this powerful hormone previously, in my book *The Domestic Church: Room by Room*, and about how it relates to mother–child bonding. This same hormone comes into play in the reward center of the brain of a tween, teen, or college-aged person. A hug lasting twenty seconds or more or a kiss can trigger this euphoric hormone, giving the person involved the impression (often false) that the person whom they are kissing or hugging is trustworthy and exceptional.

We know too that teens are more apt to act on their immature feelings and emotions than on any sort of good judgment, especially those who have not been raised with Christian faith and values. Neuroscience tells us that the reasoning part of the brain, the frontal lobe, is not high-functioning in adolescence. That fact coupled with oxytocin can lead to sex.

Young junior-high and high-school kids may be tempted to experiment with drugs, alcohol, or sex to try to fit in. And college kids living away from home are most likely thoroughly exposed to a campus culture of permissiveness.

How will they cope? What lifestyle will they choose? We hope and pray that the strong Christian foundation of prayer and values we have built for them will fare them well. Our prayers for strength and good judgment for them will aid them, no doubt. An openness to communicate with them about their concerns and yours will get an indispensable dialogue going between you.

"Mom, I'm Pregnant"
What do you do when your unwed daughter tells you she's pregnant? What about when your son tells you he has gotten his girlfriend pregnant?

On what would seem like an otherwise ordinary day, one autumn morning the text message came in: "Mom and Dad, we need your help and support. Katie is pregnant." Julia and Matthew's son Brad and his girlfriend, Katie, were texting from the parking lot of an OB doctor. They had just received test results showing that Katie was pregnant. The two young twenty- and twenty-two-year-olds were devastated and frightened, partially because Katie's father had already suspected something was up and had threatened to throw Katie out or to insist that she get an abortion—and also because Brad knew his parents expected much more of him.

Julia and Matthew weren't put off by the fact that they were receiving this life-changing news through a text message. They realized that Brad wanted them to know immediately and also desperately needed to know he'd have their support. Even so, Julia cried and asked Matthew, "Oh, my goodness! How will they be able to handle this?" These Catholic parents knew that abortion was not an option, and so they would do all they could to convince their son and his girlfriend to keep their baby. They hardly knew Katie, but they were aware that she had had another child out of wedlock. Katie lived with her two-year-old son, Kevin, and her father, with whom she had a strained relationship. Her mother had died during a heart-transplant surgery the day Kevin was born. This young lady had already suffered more than her share of heartache.

Julia's head was spinning after reading the text message. This was not supposed to happen! She had expected her son to finish college, get engaged, get married, and *then* have children. She always dreamed of dancing at Brad's wedding one day. Now what would they do? As she snapped out of her momentary rumination, her thoughts turned to first things first: They had to save their grandchild!

Later that day, Brad and his parents sat down together to hash it all out. "We told him we were disappointed and very concerned—he hadn't finished school, and he was only working part-time. How would he support a child?" Julia and Matthew told Brad that they couldn't make the decision for them but that they would help in any way they could *if* Brad and Katie chose to have the baby. Next, Julia and Matthew agreed that Katie and her son Kevin could move in with them since her father was increasingly hostile and threatening. There would be no sleeping together. Brad would move out of his bedroom and upstairs with his two brothers. Katie and Kevin would use Brad's room. Somehow they would manage, even though Matthew had been out of work for almost two years and Julia was working long hours to try to make up for it.

The transition was difficult for everyone. This all-male household (with the exception of Julia) was not accustomed to a young female in the home and certainly not used to a crying and energetic two-year-old. After a while, though, things started to click, and some interesting things happened. Brad's brothers began enjoying having Kevin around, who could be quite amusing. Julia and Matthew coaxed Katie out of her room and encouraged her to be less antisocial and more involved with the household. Katie began to enjoy the many interactions that transpire in a functional family. The brothers became more accepting of the changes in their home and more comfortable with Katie, even gently admonishing her when she reached for a brownie before a balanced breakfast.

Despite the challenges, Julia feels that it is a huge learning experience for everyone. She feels her other sons are gaining important life lessons from this after observing the difficulties that go along with doing things in an improper order. Hopefully, they will choose the right approach to dating, marriage, and starting a family. "Every day I thank God for Katie and Kevin," Julia says, "even though this is not exactly how I expected it to be." She is very excited that she and Matthew will be welcoming their grandson before long. Brad and Katie have been making plans to get married. "We couldn't be more proud about Brad's stepping up to his responsibilities," she added, "doing everything I would hope he would do for his girlfriend."

Julia is glad that she was blessed with an extra dose of patience and flexibility to handle everything. "I have faith that it's all going to work out—a little at a time, little steps." She believes God has given her the grace to say, "I wouldn't change this at all; I accept it totally."

Facing the Dark Realities of Contemporary Life

As I've mentioned throughout this book, modern technology can be a blessing or a curse. We can learn so much about our faith and be connected with like-minded people through modern media. But there's also a dark side to technology that we have to be aware of.

Janie was a happily married wife with three young children and was active in her parish. She received the shock of her life one day when she happened upon numerous love notes from her husband on her family computer. But these notes were not to her, they were to a long-lost "love" her husband had traced through the Internet.

Janie's husband later confessed that he had dabbled in Internet sex and then felt drawn to finding a lover from his past. This family is currently broken in two following the ugly divorce that ensued. They are in the midst of picking up the shards of their lives, which were torn apart by deceit, lust, sin, and an improper use of technology.

The statistics are alarming. Even back in 2003, "the Internet was a significant factor in two out of three divorces."[3] One night, as I was about to turn off my computer after a long day of work, an instant message from a woman I knew popped up on Facebook.

"Donna-Marie, do you have a minute?"

I was exhausted, but dear Mother Teresa's words rang in my ears: "Real love is when it hurts."

"Sure," I responded, "what's up?"

The woman proceeded to tell me that she was saddened about her husband's addiction to pornography. Well, that "minute" turned into an hour as I tried to help as best I could, encouraged her to speak about it to a holy priest, and promised my continued prayers.

Sadly, this woman's problem is not at all rare. Pornography is an enormous business! According to Family Safe Media, "the pornography industry is larger than the revenues of the top technology companies combined: Microsoft, Google, Amazon, eBay, Yahoo!, Apple, Netflix, and EarthLink."[4] Countless people are addicted to porn, and it's been encroaching on family life for quite some time now.

"Every second 28,258 Internet users are viewing pornography."[5] By the time you read this, that number will most likely have skyrocketed. It's a vile evil tearing families apart—we need to pray.

Kids Leaving the Faith

What do you do if your son or daughter suddenly refuses to go to Mass or even expresses that he or she is an atheist? Numerous mothers I speak with tell me how they are saddened that an older child has left the faith, some searching for something else, some turning their back on God altogether. It can occur at some point after a "child" leaves the nest, perhaps to go off to college. Some believe the anti-God mentality at most colleges is the culprit. No matter how it happens, it's an agonizing sword straight through the heart of a faithful Christian mother.

One Catholic mom, Cheryl, shared with me that her sixteen-year-old daughter, Jenny, decided to stop going to Mass after she made her confirmation.

Cheryl was baffled and thoroughly upset at this new turn of events. "We are Catholics who practice our faith by weekly participation at Mass as a family. Individually, I try to receive Jesus on a daily basis as much as I can," she said.

"It has been an ongoing issue," Cheryl explained. "Both my husband and I have remained firm—she must attend Mass." Cheryl thinks the public high school where her daughter is a student is part of the issue. "She does not really have the peer support that she may need to support her practice of and living the faith," Cheryl observed. Jenny has also complained that there are no other teens at many of the Masses.

"I think that my daughter, in her adamant vocalization against Catholicism, is attempting to define herself in her own way," Cheryl surmised. As hard as it is to deal with, Cheryl fuels herself with strength from holy Mother Church. "It is my hope and prayer," she said, "that because of the foundation upon which she has been raised, in time and with maturity she will claim Catholicism as her own—not because she has been brought up that way but because she recognizes the beauty and pearl of great price that has been planted within by her heavenly Father, who loves her so very much."

We can earnestly pray that all the Jennys out there will find their way back home to the Church. We have to believe that our prayers and the foundation of faith we have built for our own children will certainly stay with them. We must hope, pray, and trust!

Facing Contradictions

The lives of faithful Catholic mothers are full of contradictions. Frequently we deal with those who don't understand our commitment to parent our children in line with the magisterium of the Church. We are at times mocked, ridiculed, criticized, and labeled "overprotective" or "fanatical"—all because we deeply care for our children's eternal souls.

We are given unsolicited "birth control" advice by those who don't understand our openness to life. These arrows aimed at us won't harm us when we keep our eyes upward and we keep our hearts open to God's amazing love for us. His grace will see us through.

St. Josephine Bakhita, who was born in Sudan, kidnapped by slave traders, terribly abused, and treated as an outcast because she was black, was finally freed from a life of slavery and became a Catholic nun. Before she died, she said that if she were to see her tormentors again she would kneel before them, kiss them, and thank them because all of the suffering ultimately brought her to God.

There are far too many tough issues mothers face to include here. We may never understand the suffering and pain we are asked to endure, at least until we pass from this life on to the next. Despite the paucity of clear reasons, we should entrust it all to God now and ask him to sanctify it all. All the "splinters from the cross" we bear help to pave the way to heaven for our family when we loosen our control and pray for God's grace. Let's not waste our suffering.

REFLECTION

Do you allow the weariness of life and its challenges to weigh you down? What opportunities for grace might be hiding within them? Can you offer them to God? How can his grace enable you to approach your challenging situations differently?

Think of the women you know who have more than their fair share of troubles. What can you do to lend a hand and ease their burdens?

A PRAYER FOR THE JOURNEY

Dear Lord, please assist me through all the trials of life. Please grant me the grace, strength, and courage to deal with all I face each day during my Catholic mothering. Mother Mary, please pray for my family and families everywhere so that they will turn to your Son and you. Amen.

Motherly Joy

Joy is a net of love by which you can catch souls.

—Bl. Teresa of Calcutta

I'LL NEVER FORGET SITTING AT my kitchen table one evening surrounded by my husband and children. Many friends and relatives had joined us for a birthday celebration. Suddenly, I became so utterly aware of being at the heart of an incredible moment. I realized something in a way I had never before—that all those people who were gathered together could have been there only because I had answered "Yes" to God so all my children could come into being. The awareness I experienced was extremely profound and pierced straight through my heart. I quietly took it all in, secretly beaming inside with a joy difficult to express even now.

I knew without a doubt that God was showing me something phenomenal, an insight that every mother can reflect in her own heart: Our "Yes" to God regarding our openness to new life indeed changes history! And so, of course, does our "No" to him. That profound awareness of a mother's ability to change and create history has stayed with me. I suppose you can liken my experience to Frank Capra's classic movie *It's a Wonderful Life,* to the scene where George Bailey (played by James Stewart)—who had come to the conclusion that his life was not worth living—emphatically realizes through the help of his "guardian angel," Clarence, that the whole world would have been dramatically changed had he not been born.[1]

Our lives are so rich! We actively strive, we search, and we hope to unearth the deep meaning in our vocation of motherhood. Each day is extraordinary, no matter how mundane it can sometimes seem. A multiplicity of blessings is mysteriously hidden within the tiny details of day-to-day family life. With each response of love we are brought closer to our heavenly reward.

"In the encounter with the Samaritan woman at the well," Pope Benedict XVI has told us, "the topic of Christ's 'thirst' stands out in particular. It culminated in his cry on the Cross 'I thirst' (John 19:28). This thirst, like his weariness, had a physical basis. Yet Jesus, as St. Augustine says further, 'thirsted for the faith of that woman,' as he thirsted for the faith of us all." [2]

It's a good thing our Lord comes to meet us on-the-go mothers at the "well" of prayer just as he met the Samaritan woman in John 4. St. Augustine spoke about that historic meeting. He explained that Jesus is actually the first to seek us, and he finds us as we are busy drawing our water (see John 4:7). To a busy mother, this means that our Lord finds you in your housekeeping and mothering right in your domestic church! He is present with us and reminds us that he longs for our love; he thirsts for us.

I am reminded of a time when I was going to meet my husband for Mass. Dave was coming from his shop after a messy job and I was to bring him clean clothes to change into. As I pulled into the church parking lot, my heart sank. I had forgotten his shoes. Nonetheless, Dave at least changed his clothes. Just before Mass began, an usher came over and whispered to me, "Do you want to bring up the gifts?" I consider it an honor to bring up the gifts that will be consecrated into the Body and Blood of Jesus Christ, but this time I hesitated for half a second before responding, "Uh, yes, thanks, Jim." So, at the Offertory, we walked up the aisle to the altar carrying the gifts, my husband wearing his shamefully grubby sneakers and me feeling a bit embarrassed but smiling inside. Our loving God meets us where we're at, I mused. He wants us, dirty sneakers and all!

In his book *Go in Peace*, Pope John Paul II spoke about what it means to be a Christian in the modern world. Regarding the family he said:

In fact, the family is called the Church in miniature, "the domestic church," a particular expression of the Church through the human experience of love and common life. Like the Church, the family ought to be a place where the gospel is transmitted and from which the gospel radiates to other families and to the whole of society.

Catholic parents must learn to form their family as this domestic Church, a Church in the home where God is honored, his law is respected, prayer is a normal event, virtue is transmitted by word and example, and everyone shares the hopes, the problems, and the sufferings of everyone else. All this is not to advocate a return to some outdated style of human living; it is rather a return to the roots of human development and human happiness.[3]

We mothers are given the power and grace to return to those holy roots!

Let's pause often to enjoy the joys and blessings galore that fill our lives. Mothers pass on beautiful traditions to future generations through their faith, hope, and love. They create new ones too as they love their family to heaven! Treasure your all-embracing journey—your prayers and love change history!

> "Let us keep the joy of loving Jesus ever burning in your heart, and share this joy with others."
>
> —Bl. Teresa of Calcutta[4]

REFLECTION

Do you endeavor to pass on the joy in your life to others? List some of the ways.

Even amid the busyness of your life, you can pause to ponder and pray and to thank God for the wonders of his gifts to mothers. What are some of the specific gifts you are thankful for?

A PRAYER FOR THE JOURNEY

Oh, dear Lord, you light up my life with joys untold by gifting me with the vocation of motherhood. Please continue to guide me and grant me your graces so that I may please you always. Dear Mother Mary, be a Mother to me always as I embrace my vocation and usher my family toward heaven. Amen.

N o t e s

Introduction
1. Fulton J. Sheen, *Life Is Worth Living* (San Francisco: Ignatius, 1999).

Chapter One: Blessed With Little Souls
1. John Paul II, *Gratissimam Sane* (1994) 11; John Paul II, *Evangelium Vitae* (1995), 43.
2. John Paul II, *Evangelium Vitae,* 43.
3. *CCC* 2366; "is on the side of life" is from *Familiaris Consortio* 30; "each and every marriage act ... of life" is from *Humanae Vitae* 11; "This particular doctrine ... marriage act" is from *Humanae Vitae,* 12 (cf. Pius XI, *Casti connubii*).
4. John Paul II, *Familiaris Consortio*; www.vatican.va.
5. *CCC* 2367; for "Called to give life ... of God," cf. Ephesians 3:14, Matthew 23:9; "Married couples ... and Christian responsibility" is from *Gaudium et Spes,* 2.
6. John Paul II, *Familiaris Consortio,* no. 32.
7. John Paul II, *Familiaris Consortio,* no. 32.
8. John Paul II, *Familiaris Consortio,* no. 6.
9. *CCC* 2366, quoting *Humanae Vitae,* 11.
10. *CCC* 2366, quoting *Humanae Vitae,* 11.
11. *CCC* 2368.
12. *Gaudium et Spes,* no. 51, 3; www.vatican.va.
13. Pope Paul VI, *Humanae Vitae,* II, no. 16; www.vatican.va.
14. *Mulieris Dignitatem,* 18 (italic in original).
15. Benedict XVI, general audience, October 27, 2010.
16. *Behavioral Neuroscience* 124, no. 5 (2010): pp. 695–700.
17. John Paul II, *Familiaris Consortio,* 26.

Chapter Two: Building Our Domestic Church

Epigraph: John Paul II, quoted in (London) *Observer,* January 31, 1982.

1. *CCC* 1666.

2. *Evangelium Vitae,* 92; in the Vatican document, a note attached to the quoted text ("as the fruit … flows from them") reads as follows: "John Paul II, Address to Participants in the Seventh Symposium of European Bishops, on the theme of 'Contemporary Attitudes towards Life and Death: a Challenge for Evangelization' (17 October 1989), No. 5: *Insegnamenti* XII, 2 (1989), 945. Children are presented in the Biblical tradition precisely as God's gift (cf. *Ps* 127:3) and as a sign of his blessing on those who walk in his ways (cf. *Ps* 128:3–4)."

3. Benedict XVI, General Audience, Wednesday, February 7, 2007.

4. *CCC* 1661, cf. Council of Trent: DS 1799.

5. *CCC* 1606.

6. *CCC* 1608.

7. *CCC* 1608.

8. Malcolm Muggeridge, *A Gift for God: Mother Teresa of Calcutta* (New York: Harper and Row, 1975).

9. Mother Teresa of Calcutta, *Words to Love By* (Notre Dame, Ind.: Ave Maria, 1989).

Chapter Three: A Mother's Never-Ending Prayer

1. Peter Seewald, *Light of the World* (San Francisco: Ignatius, 2010).

2. John A. Hardon, "Mental Prayer Is for Everyone," The Real Presence Association, http://www.therealpresence.org/archives/Prayer/Prayer_062.htm.

3. John Henry Newman, http://www.thepapalvisit.org.uk (Home / 2010 Visit / Papal Visit Resources / Parish Resources / Prayer).

4. Mother Teresa, address at National Prayer Breakfast, February 3, 1994.

Chapter Four: First and Foremost Educator

Epigraph: John Paul II, *Familiaris Consortio,* 36.

1. Paul VI, *Gravissimum Educationis* 3, as quoted by John Paul II in *Familiaris Consortio* (1981), 36.
2. Paul VI, *Gravissimum Educationis* 3, as quoted in *CCC* 2221, where the phrase "role of parents in education" is italicized.
3. *CCC* 2223; italic in original; the phrase "material and instinctual … spiritual ones" is from John Paul II, *Centesimus Annus* 36.2.
4. John A. Hardon, *Modern Catholic Dictionary* (Bardstown, Ky.: Eternal Life, 2000).
5. Hardon, *Modern Catholic Dictionary.*
6. *Telegraph,* "Technology and Digital Media," July 2010.
7. http://internet-filter-review.toptenreviews.com/internet-pornography-statistics.html.
8. "Sexting: Shockingly Common Among Teens," CBS News, Jan. 15, 2009.
9. The National Campaign to Prevent Teen and Unplanned Pregnancy, http://www.thenationalcampaign.org.
10. For more tips and information, see http://www.thenationalcampaign.org/sextech/PDF/SexTech_Summary.pdf.
11. *New York Times,* March 4, 2008.
12. Matt Richtel, "Attached to Technology and Paying a Price," *New York Times,* June 6, 2010.
13. EWTN News, October 16, 2010.

Chapter Five: Mothering Our Daughters and Sons

Epigraph: Crossroads Initiative, http://www.crossroadsinitiative.com.

1. MSN.com, http://health.msn.com/kids-health/are-bratz-dolls-too-sexy.
2. MSN.com, http://health.msn.com/kids-health/are-bratz-dolls-too-sexy.

3. MSN.com, http://health.msn.com/kids-health/are-bratz-dolls-too-sexy.

4. Chastity.com, http://chastity.com/chastity-qa/stds/prevention/what-do-you-think-about-new-hpv-; and National Cancer Institute, http://www.cancer.gov/cancertopics/factsheet/Prevention/HPV-vaccine.

5. Ask the Mediatrician, July 12, 2010, http://cmch.typepad.com/mediatrician/2010/07/how-does-pornography-impact-boys-ideas-about-women-and-relationships.html.

6. Ask the Mediatrician, July 12, 2010.

7. *Sunday Times,* January 24, 2010.

8. *Sunday Times,* January 24, 2010.

9. *Sunday Times,* January 24, 2010.

Chapter Six: Dealing With Demands for Perfection

1. CNN.com, http://articles.cnn.com/2007-03-15/health/BK.girls.body.image_1_body-image-middle-school-girls-dads-daughters?_s=PM:HEALTH.

2. National Mental Health Information Center, www.health.gov/nhic.

3. John Paul II, *Mulieris Dignitatem,* 30 (italic in the original); in the English version at www.vatican.va, the text reads, "*Woman can only hand,*" but in most sources "hand" is rendered as "find."

4. John Paul II, *Mulieries Dignitatem,* 31 (italic in the original).

Chapter Seven: The Blessed Mother as Our Model for Holiness

1. Mother Teresa of Calcutta, *Heart of Joy* (Ann Arbor, Mich.: Servant, 1987).

2. *CCC* 2673.

3. John Paul II, *Rosarium Virginis Mariae,* October 2002.

4. John Paul II, *Rosarium Virginis Mariae.*

5. *CCC* 2679.

6. "Regina Coeli (Queen of Heaven)," *The Catholic Encyclopedia*, New Advent, http://www.newadvent.org/cathen/12718b.htm.

Chapter Eight: Dealing With the Really Difficult Stuff
1. Donna-Marie Cooper O'Boyle, "Living Proof: Through the Ultrasound Initiative, Knights Help Pregnancy Centers to Save Lives," *Columbia* magazine, January 2011, p.8.
2. *National Review Online,* December 19, 2006.
3. American Academy of Matrimonial Lawyers in 2003, www.divorcewizards.com.
4. Family Safe Media, www.familysafemedia.com.

Chapter Nine: Motherly Joy
Epigraph: Mother Teresa of Calcutta, *A Gift for God: Prayers and Meditations* (New York: HarperCollins, 1996).
1. Frank Capra, director and producer, *It's a Wonderful Life,* 1946.
2. Benedict XVI, "Angelus," March 27, 2011, www.vatican.va
3. John Paul II, *Go in Peace: A Gift of Enudring Love* (Chicago: Loyola, 2003), p. 150.
4. Mother Teresa to the author, letter, March 7, 1989.

Donna-Marie Cooper O'Boyle is a Catholic wife and mother of five. Host and creator of the EWTN series *Everyday Blessings for Catholic Moms*, she's been a catechist for more than twenty-five years as well as an internationally known speaker, award-winning journalist, and best-selling author of numerous Catholic books, including *Catholic Prayer Book for Mothers*, *The Domestic Church: Room by Room*, *Grace Café: Serving Up Recipes for Faithful Mothering*, *Mother Teresa and Me: Ten Years of Friendship*, *Catholic Saints Prayer Book*, *The Heart of Motherhood*, *Prayerfully Expecting: A Nine Month Novena for Mothers to Be*, and *A Catholic Woman's Book of Prayers*. Donna-Marie's work can be found in several magazines and publications, on the Internet, and on her many blogs. Learn more at www.donnacooperoboyle.com.